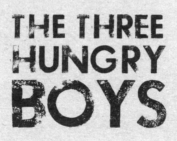

THE THREE
HUNGRY
BOYS

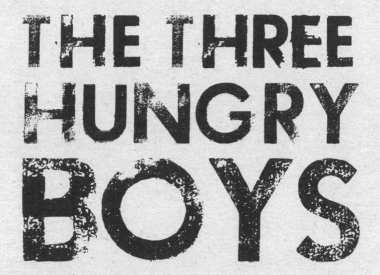

THE THREE HUNGRY BOYS

HOW TO CATCH, TRAP, FORAGE & GENERALLY BLAG YOUR WAY TO SURVIVAL IN THE WILD

TREVOR BRINKMAN
TIM CRESSWELL & THOM HUNT

SHORT BOOKS

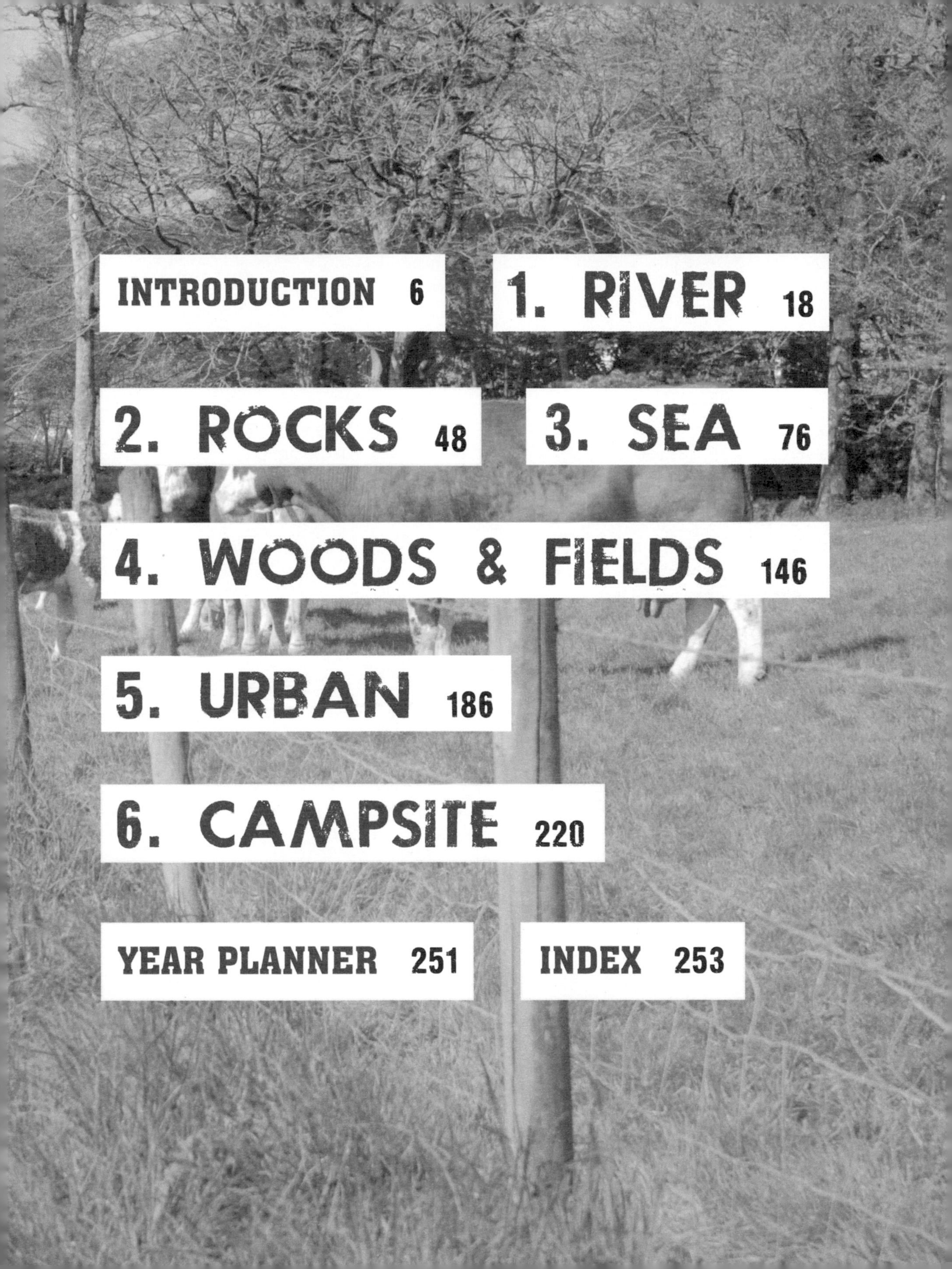

INTRODUCTION

This book is the result of what happened when three best friends left their wallets – and trepidation – at home for a month.

FOR TWO SUMMERS now, we have taken up a challenge by Channel 4 to travel around Britain for four weeks with no money – and not just to survive during this time but actually to enjoy ourselves too. We managed 30 days without spending a penny (not like that) and enjoyed (nearly) every minute of it – first in Scotland, and more recently in South-West England. This book aims to share our collective knowledge – not only of how to survive but also of how to enjoy all that's on offer just outside your own front door.

Our survival wasn't down to the fact that we are experts, although Tim does have his cycling proficiency qualification. Lots of the knowledge we needed just came from experiences and adventures that we have had over the last 20-something years, as well as what we have picked up from books and from our favourite outdoor TV heroes. Add to this our collective knowledge from studying Marine Biology at Uni, and we had enough to get by.

Luckily for you, this means you can learn from our mistakes, which is good because for every one of our successes there were many, many failures. So you won't need to eat salty rice, get tearful when lobsters escape from your pot or get soaked when your shelter collapses in the middle of the night. Rather, we hope that by the end of the book, you will know exactly what to do when you go on an adventure of your own. And, if you do find yourself on a deserted beach, you'll be able to start a roaring fire, build a lobster pot and tie a spiffing bow line.

Now, just a quick note on how to use this book. We've divided it into sections that relate to the different environments you might find yourself in on your adventure. As we think it is unlikely that you will be alone in the Arctic or stranded with nothing but a parachute in the Amazon, we've chosen environments you will encounter on a typical British adventure. Each section contains information about the animals and plants that live there and, more importantly, which of those you can eat! There is also a bit on how to keep yourself comfortable and, even more importantly, entertained. We've also thrown in for good measure some facts, anecdotes and other extras that we think might be useful on your travels. You may even want to put us right or ask us further questions on some of this and, by the power of the internet, you can do this at **www.3hungryboys.com**.

Ultimately, what we would really like is for this book to inspire you to go on an adventure of your own – and to use some of the knowledge you find tucked away in these pages to help you. Although, as fans of improvisation ourselves, we'll understand if you decide to modify our tips for your own particular adventure. That said, we should now state for the record that using a tin of baked beans as a hammer will never produce good results. At best you'll end up with a slightly bent nail or tent peg and a dented can; at worst you'll be coated head to toe in tomato sauce. Trust us: we have tried many times.

So, armed with the right knowledge, some basic equipment and an eagerness for eating potentially unknown foods, we bid you good luck in your quest to master the outdoors. Our journey so far has been amazing: learning something new each time, and, as Trevor says, getting it wrong – lots!

HELLO MY NAME IS TREVOR BRINKMAN, and I am exactly one third of the Three Hungry Boys. I was born in Amsterdam in May, 1981, and spent the next four years in Holland before moving to England. This was just long enough to learn Dutch, which was nice but not particularly helpful, as outside of Holland no one really speaks it. We moved to London in 1985, where there were no bikes, clogs, raw herring or liquorice and the cheese was of a very mediocre standard. Aged 11, I moved with my mother and brothers to Stroud which is now a place for the rich and famous but back then, due to something to do with ley lines, attracted a very unique kind of person – one that has a mind open to the cosmos and usually several rebellious children in tow. On my first day at new school I heard my soon-to-be-good-friend Geoff telling our tutor exactly where he could put his xylophone beater. This was a very different place to my last school. To make matters worse, I now had a fringe much like Alex James in the Britpop years, but a few years too early. With my stupid hair, I was an instant target and if I hadn't grown to be about four inches taller than everyone else in the summer I might never have survived. But survive I did.

After A levels, I started to move around a lot, owing to some serious indecision in regards to 'the plan'. This involved Amsterdam, the Isle of Wight, university with Tim and Thom, a year in Australia in search of 'the plan', Amsterdam for another year, a degree in industrial design and now the Three Hungry Boys – and that is me, in a nutshell.

T
R
E
V
O
R

I'M TIM CRESSWELL, I'm 29 and currently live on the Devon-Cornwall border in Plymouth. In spring 2009, at the end of a grim, dark winter, Hunty (that's Thom to you) and I had a conversation about counting your life in summers. If we lived to the age of 80, then we only had another 50 or so years to enjoy on this beautiful earth! (Bit morbid, but look where it got us.) We decided we'd plan a trip away for the summer; spearfishing, surfing and generally having a blast. Later that night, in bed and very nearly asleep, I thought, 'You know what. I bet someone somewhere would be up for giving us a camera and making something of this.' I then thought that the best person, with access to the right gear and a love for this kind of thing, was Hugh Fearnley-Whittingstall. So I wrote a bit of a cheeky email to river cottage.net about lending us a camera and letting us film the trip. To our total amazement, we got a reply, and the rest, as they say, is history...

I'm a 'do everything' kind of person and try to fill every minute with 60 seconds of worthwhile stuff, which partly comes from growing up with two awesome brothers; there was always someone to mess around with when I was a kid. I wouldn't change a single thing about my upbringing.

I met Thom and Trevor in 2000, at university, studying Marine Biology, where we lived together on and off for several years. I now work as a biology teacher and love the subject and the immense challenge and reward of working with young people. I am a closet creative and vent my frustrations by writing music and taking photographs. My family instilled in me the joys of making music with other people at a very young age, and I have done so ever since, playing in several bands, orchestras, jam sessions and the like. My Nan, Audrey, taught me Gilbert and Sullivan and my Great Uncle and Granddad got me into playing the trombone in jazz and big bands. Nowadays, I play guitar and write music for a few bands, so it's all a little bit cooler (although I do occasionally have a blow on the trombone on mates' recordings). I co-run a photography business too, shooting all sorts of photos – fashion, music, portraits – for a vast range of people and companies.

I'm a big believer in the phase 'know thyself'. In my opinion, you have to be fixed on what it is you want and get there any way you can. I hear people talking all the time about being disappointed with their lot. No one will ever come along and offer you your dream; you've got to make it happen for yourself.

THoM 😊

I'M THOM HUNT. I'm 29 years old and I was a fish in a past life. I have spent most of my life involved in activities to do with fish. Coarse, sea or fly fishing, you name it, if it has anything to do with outsmarting a fish, I'll do it. A quick look at my collection of 44 different rods should confirm this if you're in any doubt. I studied Marine Biology at university, where I met and lived with Dumb and Dumber, who have been my sidekicks ever since. I'm a PADI scuba instructor and a sponsored competition angler. My favourite hobby is spearfishing, and my favourite food is barbequed barracuda. I have travelled the world in pursuit of shark species because they absolutely fascinate me. I am a hugely competitive person, and can never turn a challenge down. I love hunting and spent most of the summers of my childhood on my grandparent's farm, helping out and trying to shoot rabbits for dinner! In my opinion, reality and jobs are overrated. If you have an idea or passion, just go for it. Trips like the ones we have been lucky enough to go on are, I believe, the adventures that make up 'a life well lived'. Oh yes, one more thing. There is nothing I love more than spending time with my friends. And that's pretty much me. Tight Lines!

THE EMAIL TIM WROTE TO RIVER COTTAGE (SPELLING MISTAKES AND ALL!), WHICH LAUNCHED THE THREE HUNGRY BOYS' FIRST INCREDIBLE TRIP

From: timcresswell@mac.com

To: info@rivercottage.net

Subject: hello

▶ Attachments: *none*

Hi River Cottage (and a manifestation of the big man Hugh himself.)

I am writing with hope and anticipation that befits only the best of us that have followed River Cottage from A cook on the Wild Side (and have subsequently been bought all of your box sets. So as I see it, I have benefited you with over £100 pounds worth of business, so I'm hoping you may at least hear me out).

I am a photographer, musician and devout spear fisherman from Plymouth, Devon and would like some help. Myself and two friends are planning a trip in a bid for a self-sufficient holiday. In the light of the credit crunch, we're planning a low budget trip. Our mission is to catch, work for, trap, shoot, pillage and generally pimp out our collective knowledge of the wild life (all of us are marine biology graduates) in exchange for food. The trip should take us about a month. Myself (Tim) and my two best friends (Thom and Trevor) have been spear fishing for a good while and our favorite spot actually featured on the River Cottage fish program at Trevone about Pilchards vs Sardines (incidently Hugh, if you're readin', you used my mussel-collecting bucket and knife with the tip missing as you stayed at my mate Lizzie's parents' house, Lagos - old phone on the wall and duffel coats in the hall. Been naked there a lot). With our spear guns, an air-rifle (!), some fishing rods and lobbo pots we want to see what we can catch. Trevor is retraining as a Graphic Designer and has filmed and will appear on a BBC 2 production based in Paris called 'Design School' (working title) in January with Felipe Stark. Thom is a national standard match fisherman and builder, and could catch a tuna in a puddle.

All we really want to do is pitch our idea to someone who may want to broadcast it in return for the loan of some camera gear, a little money and some travel equipment.

I hope this finds it's way to someone who will read it and maybe pass it on to someone who could do something with it.

In blind eagerness I wait for a return email.

Yours Sincerely,
Tim Cresswell.

OUR HEROES

David Attenborough

Jacques Cousteau

Thor Heyerdahl

Tim's Dad

Didier Noirot

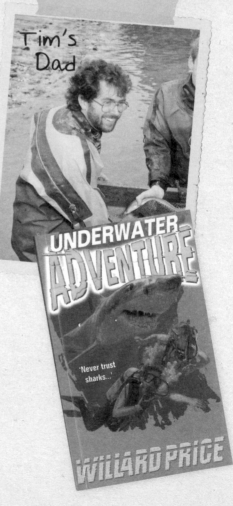

UNDERWATER ADVENTURE

'Never trust sharks...'

WILLARD PRICE

TREVOR'S HEROES

My grandmother used to insist that I watched educational documentaries when I went to stay with her with my brothers. Luckily for us there was a Dutch channel that used to broadcast natural history programmes and amongst these was a series following **Jacques Cousteau** and his voyages around the world on his ship, *Calypso*. This Frenchman and his motley crew fascinated me. They had futuristic equipment, which they used to navigate previously unexplored parts of the world; it was Jacques Cousteau who invented the first aqualung that led to today's scuba diving equipment. As well as all their cool equipment and adventures they also all wore these great red knitted hats!

When I was younger I read a lot, in fact, I read as if my life depended on it. We had a small library at my first school and I think that at some point I got the impression that I had to read every single book in it before I left school. I'd borrow four books at a time and read them on the way home, when I got home, at the dinner table and any spare moment I got. It was during this phase that I discovered the books of **Willard Price**. Every story basically had the same plot, involving Hal and his younger brother. The core message was that if you were honest and true to your beliefs, with a bit of hard work, anything was possible. Cheaters never prospered and the world was black and white. I recently tried to find out a bit more about the author and it turns out that the books were largely based on his own experiences as he travelled across the world writing articles for *National Geographic*. He also did a bit of spying during the Second World War, which just makes him cooler in my opinion.

The last on my list of influencers is a man who is a leader in design and has been hugely influential in what I believe to be world-changing projects: **Yves Behar**, founder of Fuse Project. The design projects he has been involved with range from luxury consumer products to mass packaging but the work I respect the most is the One Laptop Per Child (OLPC) project. The project attempted to produce a laptop that could be made for $100 and the aim was to ensure that children in developing countries could have the same opportunities as those in the developed world. The resulting laptop eventually ended up costing $150 but it was a stroke of genius: rugged, robust, dust- and water-proof; it could be used outside in the sun, it could form local networks and most importantly the client (children) loved it.

TIM'S HEROES

David Attenborough definitely tops my list. His calm and eloquent approach to every wild situation inspired me to learn about the natural world – and never fails to make me want to sell all my belongings on ebay, go off around the world and see everything for myself. The sardine run up the west coast of Africa, the miraculous migratory journey of wild Alaskan salmon and the killer whales feeding on seals in North America are my personal Attenborough favourites. Luckily, I have

the box sets of all his programmes on DVD so I still have my worldly possessions and am living in the UK. But there's always the option!

Ray Mears is every modern man's hero and if you find someone who denies it, they are either lying or don't know who he is, but before him, Sunday afternoon television was dominated by the wonderful programmes of the **Bush Tucker Man**, **Les Hiddins**. Long before Bear or Hugh were eating all sorts of dodgy stuff, this guy was the king of survival, and finding nasty grubs to eat in the wilderness was his forte. After foraging through a rotten log, he would pull out a grub the length of your finger and as fat as your big toe and, without hesitation, bite the thing in half, spilling its guts all down his chin. For an 11-year-old boy, this was about as good as TV could get...

My Dad. My very first memories of my dad were of him in his Land Rover Defender, sporting a wax jacket and smelling slightly of fish. For a very long time – as I'm sure many sons did too – I thought my Dad played cricket for England and football for Manchester United. (I found out later that he occasionally used to play five-a-side, and in the summer, 20-over matches for his work.) My dad is a hero: bringing up three sons, and working hard to ensure we had the things he didn't. He has always had a love for fish and fishing, taking me at every available opportunity. It must have been bitterly disappointing for him to find out that I am not a very good fisherman, not very good at all. I am so bad in fact that even being given an already set-up rod in an already ground-fed swim in a foolproof lake can render me fishless.

THOM'S HEROES

I grew up watching **John Wilson**'s *Go Fishing* show on TV. He's a great all-rounder, with incredible knowledge on every aspect of angling, anywhere in the world. His famous laugh every time he hooked a fish plus his brilliant one-liners make him my fishing hero: 'We're in!'

Despite everyone telling him he was mad, **Thor Heyerdahl** was convinced that the Polynesians got to their islands by crossing the Pacific Ocean on rafts over a thousand years ago. The only way to prove it? Build a balsa wood raft and attempt to recreate the journey. Thor and five equally mad friends completed the world famous *Kon-Tiki* expedition back in 1947, and in my opinion it is the greatest adventure story ever told. Read his book; it's awesome.

I have been fortunate enough to meet the third of my heroes, and I have written about the day I met him in this very book. He is called **Didier Noirot** and he is one of the greatest underwater videographers in the world. His record speaks for itself, starting his career as a crew member on the *Calypso*, Jacques Cousteau's legendary ocean voyage boat and then going on to film the amazing, award-winning *Blue Planet* and *Planet Earth* series for the BBC.

GETTING ON OUR SOAPBOX

IN THE 19TH CENTURY, people who had something they thought was important to say would take a wooden crate to a busy road, stand on the crate and rant at people walking past. Those crates had sometimes been used to carry soap so people would call this getting on your soapbox. You can still see people doing it today at Speaker's Corner around Hyde Park in London, and often when someone is in the middle of a long monologue about this, that or the other, you can hear people whispering, 'There they go again, getting on their soapbox.'

Well, dear readers, it is time for us to get on our soapbox. We are only going to be on it for a short while and we promise that by doing this there will be no more nagging for the rest of the book. Really all that we want to do is make sure that both you and the environment you visit look the same after you have been there. The forest should still look like the forest and you should still look like you, but with a big grin on your face.

OK, so here we go: our principles for not getting hurt, hurting others or getting into trouble...

Sharp knives.

First things first: knives are sharp. Their main job is to cut things and it's usually best if these things aren't you. When handling knives make sure you are safe. If possible, keep a sheath over the knife when it isn't being used. Definitely don't run with a knife in your hand – there are too many things to trip over outside and if you fall on a knife you won't be too happy about it. Make sure that your knife is sharp and well looked after, a blunt knife is much more dangerous than a sharp one.

Guns.

We quite often use things like spear guns and air rifles to catch our dinner; they look dangerous but the truth is that in the right hands they are perfectly safe. Some key points to remember are:

- When not being used, any gun must always be unloaded.
- Never point a gun or rifle at anyone, even if it is unloaded.
- Cover sharp points when transporting spears.
- Check that you are allowed to shoot and what you are allowed to shoot before you start.

Take only as much as you need.

When foraging, it is really important to understand that what you are picking or collecting will have an impact on the environment. The plants you take have a role in their ecosystem and removing them can upset the balance. Before you begin foraging have a good think about how much you actually need to take and make sure you are sensible. Make sure too that you are allowed to take plants and animals. It can be against the law in certain areas to remove wildlife, so you need to do some research before you do so.

Only eat what you absolutely 100% know to be edible.

There is no guarantee when foraging that what you are picking is good to eat. It may just be looking a bit tired but it might also be completely inedible or dangerous. You have to use a good deal of common sense to decide whether or not you can eat a plant or mushroom for instance, and some can be lethal. The bottom line is, if you aren't 100% sure it is edible and from a good, clean, healthy source, you shouldn't eat it.

Always check that you are allowed to be where you are.

Whether foraging or camping. Don't make the mistake of wandering through someone's back garden or trekking through a nature reserve. You wouldn't like it if someone did that to you.

Always tell someone where you're going.

If something goes wrong, there will be someone who can raise the alarm when you don't return, and will know roughly where you ought to be. This is totally key.

Leave only footsteps, take only memories.

This saying basically means: minimise the impact you have on the area you visit. As much as is humanly possible, we make sure that our campsite looks the same when we leave as it did when we arrived. We also take all our rubbish with us and dispose of it properly. In fact, if you can, you should take any rubbish that others have left as well; think of it as payment for your overnight stay.

1. RIVER

BEFORE YOU GO FISHING:

UNLESS LOCAL RULES APPLY, all sea fishing is free of charge and does not require a licence – however all coarse (freshwater) fishing does require one.

There are two types of fishing licence available for coarse fishing, depending on the species you are targeting. The two types of licence cover either 'non migratory trout and coarse fish' (which include carp, pike, bream, perch etc) or 'migratory trout and salmon' (sea trout and salmon). These are available from the Environment Agency – the governing body of freshwater angling for the UK – and can be purchased at all Post Offices or online at **http://www.environment-agency.gov.uk/**.

The licences enable you to use a rod and line but you still need permission to fish waters you don't own. It's a bit like a gun licence that allows you to have and use a gun but you still need the farmer's permission to shoot on his land. If you are paying to fish private water, always check the rules, which can differ from river to river and at different times of the year.

There are also rules on what fish you are allowed to catch and keep – so don't always assume when you've got a bite on the line that you've caught your dinner! You might well have to return your fish to the water. So make sure you check carefully about the rules that apply to the particular area you are fishing in and to the fish that you are planning on catching!

'Any angler aged 12 or over, fishing for Salmon, Trout, Freshwater fish or Eels in England (except the River Tweed), Wales or the Border Esk and its tributaries in Scotland MUST have an Environment Agency rod licence.'
The Environment Agency

PIKE FISHING

CATCHING A PIKE has always been a thrilling prospect for me. They are the perfect predator, found in freshwater systems throughout the UK. They grow to huge sizes (45lb in weight and over 4 foot in length), and with their rows of large, sharp teeth they have something of a legendary status. I have heard of pike so big that they have attacked ducks and even dogs in the water. I have personally been in the process of catching a smaller pike when a much larger one has risen from the depths, flashing its teeth, and clamping down on the smaller pike, before turning with an explosive thrash of water and heading off, snapping my line and leaving me standing on the river bank in stunned silence. Pike are very exciting to catch; they fight hard and can make one of the best freshwater fish to eat. So if you're interested in testing your fishing ability, your tackle and then possibly your cooking skills, here's my foolproof guide…

THE RULES

1.

First and foremost, the old adage: location, location, location. Pike are a naturally occurring predator in many freshwater systems throughout the UK, and the chances are that your local river, lake or canal with any reasonable depth (2-3ft or more) will contain a few of these toothy critters. By far the best thing to do is to find your local fishing tackle shop and see if you can coax some of their extensive knowledge out of them – if you ask nicely, they should happily point you in the direction of a local waterway that contains pike.

2.

Keep your fishing tackle and rigs simple. When you enter a tackle shop, the range of wonderful colours, smells and gadgets is enough to leave any newcomer confused. I often think there is just as much tackle out to catch the angler as the fish.

Your best bet is: a medium/strong rod of 10-12ft, coupled with fixed spool reel loaded with a line of 10 or 12lb breaking strain. The whole set up can be bought from as little as £30. A simple rig of a sturdy, buoyant float to suspend the bait and register the bite, some small round weights to cock the float and add casting weight and a wire trace with a treble hook will do very well. (See Rigs on page 143 for a diagram.) This rig is great for presenting a small live bait whereas a simple ledger rig is best for offering dead bait. Nice and simple, very effective and it can be set up in less than 5 minutes… Easy!

3.

If I was only to pass on one piece of knowledge I have learned in my years of pike fishing, it would be that there is no better bait than live bait – a small live roach, perch or skimmer bream of a couple of ounces (around 4 inches long) is perfect. This is such an effective bait that I have caught numerous pike literally within seconds of casting. Cast the bait in, wait for the float to cock, and if there is a hungry pike in the area it will snaffle it straight away. These live baits are best caught using maggots, small sections of worm or tiny pieces of bread on a simple float set up and kept in a bucket of water or keepnet. Always take one or two dead baits though, because if you don't get any live bait you won't have anything to fish with! Good dead baits for pike include freshwater fish (the ones mentioned above, my preference is to buy them frozen from tackle shops) or even sea dead baits including mackerel, sardines and smelt. These can be purchased from supermarkets, fishmongers or good tackle shops and I would particularly recommend smelt, a small, silver fish that oddly smells of cucumbers... Incidentally, although you will catch less pike on dead baits, they do tend to be larger fish, so if you fancy the chance of a monster give these a go.

4.

Remember, according to UK law, any pike over 65cm can't be removed for eating, so if you catch a big 'un, make sure it goes back into the water to see another day.

5.

Other useful tackle items include a seat or seat box to keep yourself comfortable and transport other items including food/drink; some forceps to remove the hooks from a caught fish; a net; a rag to keep your hands clean; and maybe a few lures or spinners if you fancy a change of tactics.

6.

Watercraft is another aspect that is key for a successful catch. The best anglers always have a great sense of where the fish will be in any particular water. To catch a fish you must think like a fish! Generally on rivers, lakes and canals you should look for fish far enough away from any bank side disturbance and in a reasonable depth of water (a minimum of 2-3 feet deep). Pike are ambush predators, and their beautiful mottled green and brown markings are designed to help them blend into the weeds and reeds where they lie in wait for their next unsuspecting meal. This means that any weeds, lilies, rushes or overhanging trees you can see are always great places to find pike. They feed on smaller shoal fish so always keep your eyes peeled for large swirls and small fry scattering on the surface, and remember to ask other anglers about where they have had success. Even if they are not fishing for pike, they may be catching the shoal fish that pike feed on and where there's shoal fish, the pike will never be far away!

The least delicious fish I have ever been forced to eat.

I love fishing. Not as much as Thom who has an unhealthy obsession with the sport, but still more than lots and lots of people. My love of fishing comes from my childhood, when a tin of luncheon meat would serve firstly as good bait and then, after hours of not having caught anything but minnows and gudgeon, a satisfactory lunch. But still, I love fishing.

However, there is one childhood fishing trip to the local gravel pit that really sticks in my mind. My dad had given me a small spinning rod and a little flashing spinner. Having never caught a pike before, I didn't really know what I was up against. I actually think it was Dad who hooked the sizeable, fresh water fishy-alligator thing, before giving me the reins to pull it in. As the apex predator of the freshwater scene, the pike greedily gobbled up the spinner – a little too greedily, managing to swallow the thing halfway to its intestines.

After a few minutes of struggling to remove the hooks from deep inside the pike's mouth, Dad decided it was time to put the thing out of its misery. I still remember his annoyance and disappointment at having to kill the fish needlessly, teaching me a valuable lesson in the process. Although it would be on the menu for tea, so its death would not be totally in vain.

Sawing through the fish to create steaks and watching its tail waggle when we cut through its spine probably didn't help the situation, and, even with a light grilling and served with some spuds, I wouldn't say that I faced my pike dish with delight. I tried – really I did – to enjoy it, imagining that the poor fish could have lived to see another day if it hadn't been for me, but I still couldn't get away from one single fact: pike is pretty disgusting.

In all honesty, my pike never had much of a chance. It was fairly big and old, and had seen better days. The gravel pit we fished from had a silty bottom, which also generally affects the taste of a freshwater fish.

Putting this incident behind me, I am reliably informed that pike are, on the whole, quite edible, and recipes range from frying fillets – a chip shop favourite – to freshwater fish cakes.

gone fishing
Tim.
See above
Back with dinner.
Thom
YOU SAY TOMATO

TROUT FISHING

BEFORE THE SHOW LAST YEAR, my fly fishing skills were limited, to say the least. I had only been fly fishing a couple of times, borrowing kit from various friends, and found it difficult. Looking back now, I think it was either pure luck, determination driven by hunger, or a mixture of the two, that led me to catch my first beautiful (and delicious) 2lb brown trout. It definitely wasn't skill! That success spurred me into buying a full fly fishing kit within a week of returning home. 'Fluff-chucking', as fly fishing is known, is now up there as one of my favourite hobbies. And it just so happens that you end up with beautiful, sustainable, fresh fish for dinner at the end of it.

I am telling you this to encourage you. You see, with the right tips at your disposal, you can master the basics of trout fishing in a relatively short space of time. You'll struggle to wade through the 7,830,000 hits that Google offers under 'fly fishing for trout' to find what is really helpful. So that's what I'm here for: to refine and condense the information down to what you actually need for the best chance of success. Here is what I learnt within the space of a few months, and how I learnt it, with the result that I can now turn up at my local fishery and usually catch more than most of the other people there.

TOP TIPS FOR SUCCESS

1.

I went to my local tackle shop and spent about £100 on an outfit including rod, reel, line and a few flies, enough to get me started. I picked the owner's brains for about an hour (for free!) on local fisheries to try and flies to use, something I wouldn't have been able to do if I'd purchased my gear from the internet (key tip: local info). I did however go on the internet for two other things. I googled 'complete trout book, UK' and found a forum where existing experienced anglers repeatedly recommended two books, *The Classic Guide to Fly Fishing for Trout* by Charles Jardine and *Matching the Hatch* by Pat O'Reilly (key tip: getting not just any books but the right books). The first gave me good all-round information on history, tackle, flies and casting techniques. The second gave me a great understanding of entomology and the different bugs and flies I was trying to imitate to catch my trout.

2.

Then I went onto YouTube to get visual tips on casting styles, and went down to the park to practise casting (key tip: practise your casting on your own first). I thought it was better to get a good level of knowledge and a little bit of skill on my own, rather than paying someone to teach or explain the real basics that I could have easily – and did – get elsewhere.

3.

It's best to start on smaller, well-stocked fisheries but when you fancy a challenge there are some reservoirs that are up to 900 acres in the UK that are great for trout fishing. I went to my local fishery twice (catching nothing the first time, then one trout on the next go; hardly a great start) before booking an hour's casting lesson which was worth its weight in gold (key tip: casting lesson).

My instructor Bob also recommended some more great books from his 30 years of experience, the best being *The Pursuit of Stillwater Trout* by Brian Clarke. This was written in 1975 and sets out the author's own step by step actions that enabled him to better his results. A great read that novices can relate to.

4.

After that lesson each time I went fishing, I would make sure I chatted to the other anglers and always sought out the chap who was doing better than everyone else which was very key to improving my fly fishing (key tip: current successful methods). There is one fellow at my local fishery called Mark who I have seen catch more trout than everyone else put together, even when the lake is busy. He recommended *My Way With Trout* by Arthur Cove. I didn't know it at the time but Mr Cove was a pioneer in trout fishing and this book is not only very informative, but one of the most entertaining reads out there. Highly recommended!

While on the subject of chatting to people – maybe it's a stiff-upper-lip, British thing – but so many people refrain from asking strangers for advice. There have been times when I have caught five trout (in two hours) and everyone else on the lake has caught one at best (and been there most of the day), and even in the passing chit chat of 'afternoon, any luck?', still no one will ask what I'm doing differently. I go out on a limb and, without trying to sound like a know-it-all, mention that I'm catching on an orange blob (because it's January and there are very few bugs in the water to imitate), that I'm fishing at a depth of two to four feet (because the fish will be swimming a little deeper in January as the water is warmer where it's deeper), with a fast retrieve (because it sparks an aggressive response) and in the corners of the lake where there's a bit of ripple (because fish don't have eye lids and a ripple helps cut direct sunlight out on a sunny day, plus I've seen a few moving there). Suddenly everyone is on the orange blobs and catching! If only they'd just asked in the first place! Be sociable and polite when chatting to others and your fishing knowledge will increase massively, plus you'll probably make a few friends.

5.

Finally I got some DVDs from ebay; any with Hywel Morgan (the Welsh casting champ) are great, especially *Stillwater Fly Fishing: The Main Course* (key tip: further techniques and fly selection).

Having followed these key routes to knowledge myself, I am not necessarily the best angler, but good enough to get better results than most others who have been doing it for a much longer time, purely because I went about it a little more efficiently in a relatively short space of time. I see so many people fishing but not catching, and my fear is that they get disheartened and never return to the sport again.

MY ESSENTIAL EQUIPMENT FOR TROUT FISHING:

✳ For a starter kit, buy a 9-9.5ft rod with an AFTM rating of 6 or 7. Go for Greys or Snowbee; both are good. If money is tight, buy from ebay. Second hand rods are so much cheaper and you should be able to pick up a model only a year or two old for half its retail price.

✳ If you want to save money, save it on the reel. Cheap ones (£15) are OK and will do the job.

✳ When it comes to the line, I would suggest you buy a 'weight forward floating' line, by Snowbee XS or Cortland 444. Do not buy cheap lines, they will make life very hard. Expect to pay £30-40. This may seem expensive but it's worth it.

✳ Use a tapered leader to start with – you will get much fewer tangles. This is a continuous piece of line that starts very thick and gradually thins down.

MY TOP FLIES *(Drum roll here please)*

There are two categories of flies: lures and imitators. Lures look nothing like any food the trout would eat or encounter normally. They tend to be big with bold colours; bright yellows, oranges, pinks etc. So why do trout eat them? Well, mostly out of curiosity. Fish don't have hands so if they want to investigate something they use their mouth, much to their downfall at times when that 'something' has a hook in it. (This is true of tiger sharks too. They are notorious for having bizarre objects in their stomachs. At the Sharks Board Museum in Umhlanga, South Africa they have a cabinet holding all the strange objects found in tiger sharks during public dissections over the years. These include an industrial size can of corned beef, car registration plates – no joke, just like *Jaws!* – a tom-tom and a human skull.)

Anyway, back to trout. So brightly coloured lures can be great at catching trout but if you want a real challenge try catching them on a 'natural imitator'. This is so much more rewarding as you have to learn what type of insects hatch at different times of the day/year (which is called entomology, not to be confused – and I'm sure you wouldn't be anyway – with etymology, which is the study of the history of words, don't you know) to work out what the trout are naturally feeding on and then try and offer something that both looks and behaves like the real thing. Quite difficult, I can tell you. So, start on my two lure patterns to catch a few trout and gain some confidence, then move on to the imitators once you get the hang of it.

MY TWO FAVOURITE LURES

Fish these two shallow, in the top four feet of water, fish them quite fast and make sure your retrieve is erratic: a little tweak of the line, a long fast pull, then stop, then a short quick pull etc.

The bites are normally very positive as the trout tries to pull the rod into the water, instead of you pulling the trout out. Now get prepared for the weird names…

THE ORANGE BLOB

Size 8 or 10. Basically it's like a bit of scrunched up tinsel that wouldn't look out of place on the Christmas tree. It comes in quite a few materials but my favourite is 'fritz'. It glitters in the sun and pulses as you pull it through the water. The trout are totally confused by it, so check it out with their mouths. BIG mistake. Me -1 Trout - 0. Fish them 0-2 feet deep.

WOOLLY BUGGER

Size 8. Very large with a woolly body and a fluffy tail. Try pink, black or orange. Fish them a little deeper than the blobs at 2-4 feet. Be prepared for a few 'tugs' on the line as the fish nip the tail before fully grabbing it and hooking themselves. My favourite is pink.

NOW FOR THE NATURAL IMITATORS

DAMSEL NYMPH

Size 10-12. Imitating the damsel fly, which is the smaller relative of the well known dragon fly. A medium/large size so when seen underwater by your trout can represent quite a meal. Damsel nymphs live near the bottom of the water or around weed beds so use your Damsel Nymph fly there.

COCH-Y-BONDU

Size 12-16. A Welsh pattern that imitates little beetles.

SPENT MAYFLY

Fished on the surface, to imitate the dead or dying 'spent' fly, after it has laid its eggs (mayflies only live for one day as flies; they have no mouth parts to feed with, so they just lay their eggs, then kark it). Once cast, leave them, only occasionally twitching them. Extremely exciting fishing when there is a huge swirl in the water, as a fish rises for the bait.

GOLD RIBBED HARE'S EAR

Size 10-14. A great brown/grey/tan coloured imitation that could be mistaken for a lot of the underwater nymphs (the organisms that live underwater before growing wings and swimming to the top to 'hatch' into a fly). The great saying of 'if in doubt, put a GRHE on' is very true. Fish them anywhere from the surface to the lake bed. The best all-rounder.

BUZZER

Size 12-16. Buzzers, or Chironomids to use the proper name, start off as small worm-like larvae (ever heard of the red bloodworm?) that later hatch into small flies including midges and mosquitoes, getting their name from the irritating noise they make when flying around your lug-hole. Quite small but usually a lot of them so the trout love 'em. Fish them up to 3 feet deep and VERY slowly.

So after following these key steps, you will hopefully get a trout to take home at the end of the day. Then all you have to do is follow the gutting and filleting 'how to's, (see pages 122-125) and check out Trevor's great recipe ideas.

Happy fishing!

MAKING YOUR OWN CRAYFISH TRAP, AND TRAPPING THE LITTLE CRITTERS FOR TEA!

OVER THE LAST FEW YEARS, the American signal crayfish (*Pacifastacus leniusculus*) has invaded our precious waterways. It has brought a disease that is fast killing our native crayfish species (*Austropotamobius pallipes*). It burrows deep into river and lake banks, causing erosion, and is multiplying at such a rate that many believe our freshwater ecosystems will be affected in the long term. Crayfish have become the grey squirrel of the water world.

Unfortunately for the American signal, it tastes excellent and is great fun to catch which means we can catch them to our heart's content guilt-free. To find out where is a good local spot for crayfish, contact your nearest fishing shop, or look online for forums that should tell you where to go to guarantee success.

There are quite a few interesting ways to catch these greedy little blighters so here's some top tips for bagging a 'freshwater lobster' meal!

1.

The simplest method is just to tie your bait securely on the end of a string and cast it into the water. If you use smelly fish or meat-based bait, like an old fish head, bacon rashers or leftover bones it shouldn't take longer than 10 minutes before you get the gentle 'tug-tug' on the line. This is your cue to steadily pull the line in and basically hope the crayfish is greedy enough to hold on!

2.

The other method involves making your own contraption to catch or net the crayfish. Not only is it great fun to make something from scratch yourself or with the kids, but it is also hugely satisfying once you've caught your supper. (Up there with catching a trout on a home-tied fly.)

MAKING YOUR OWN TRAP

Back when I was about 18, I had returned to a glorious summer in the UK after travelling around Australia for 6 months. As usual, I had little money, plenty of time on my hands, a best mate who loved adventures and the blazing sunshine to enjoy. This coincided with an explosion in our local canal of the American signal crayfish. Hearing they were good to eat, my mate and I set out to 'do our bit' for Great Britain against the American invasion. We spent that whole summer on the scrounge for chicken wire, cable ties and old rope to build as many different types of traps as we could possibly imagine.

We refined our approach quite well and even got to the point where we contacted pubs in the area to see if they wanted to buy our fresh local produce as we had caught so many.

Here's what we learnt from our 'crayfish summer':

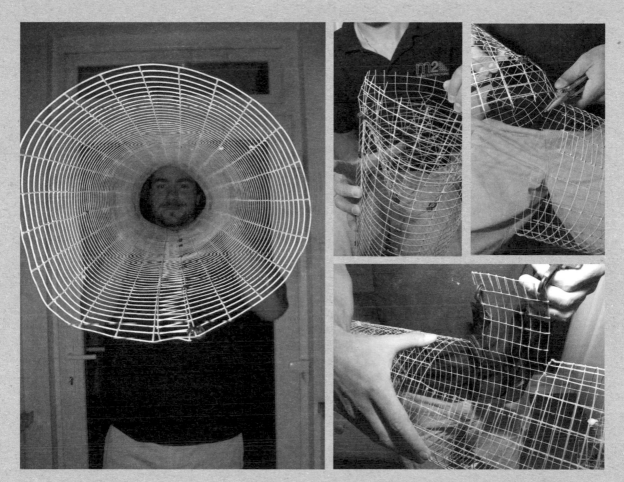

YOU WILL NEED: a sheet of chicken wire (with holes no larger than a 50p piece) approx. 3-4ft square, cable ties, wire cutters, a length of strong string or rope (say 10-15ft long) and the all important bait! (I'll cover this later.)

✳ In our experience, the shape of trap that produced the best results was a tube 2-2.5ft long with the diameter of a dinner plate, with inverted cone shapes at each end. For the cone entrances, imagine a plastic bottle with the top cut off and turned round so the pouring hole is inside the bottle. This type of shape allows the crayfish to walk from the wide area into the trap and, as it passes the narrow 'bottleneck', it falls into the main compartment where the bait is, from where it is very difficult to get out.

✳ Roll the chicken wire into a tube of about 1ft in diameter, overlapping the ends by a few inches and secure using cable ties.

✳ Now cut a baiting hatch halfway down the tube, big enough to get your hand in and the crayfish out – about six inches square should be good! Make it a square shape but leave one of the four sides uncut (the bendy wire will act as a hinge for your hatch door). Secure this using something that can undo and do up easily. We used a plastic clip from an old rucksack.

✳ Using the wire cutters snip 20-25cm from the edge of the tube towards the centre, in three equally spaced lines around the tube. Imagine the end of the tube is a circle. If you drew a 'Y' inside the circle, the three points where the 'Y' touches the wire are the three points where you should make your cuts. These will then bend inside the main tube to create your bottleneck. Make three cuts at each end so your trap has two entrances.

✸ Bend the three flaps inside and use cable wire to create a cone that has an end hole roughly the size between a ping-pong ball and a snooker ball. Too large and they can get out again! You can tie the ends by going through your hatch if that makes things easier. Be careful though as the cut wire may be sharp – you aren't going to cut your arm off but it could give you a nasty scratch.

✸ Tie your rope onto one end, looping it through the chicken wire holes, and secure with a bowline knot (see page 139 for correct knot).

✸ Now for the good bit: find a local waterway (lake, river, canal – again, ask around at a local angling shop to find one in your area) that the crayfish live in and get fishing!

✸ You can use any old meat/fish you have knocking around at home, but after trying many different types of bait, the best we found were sections of eel, the reason being that it is as tough as old boots. At first we used soft fish bait like mackerel but the first few crays would get in there and devour it all, leaving nothing to attract any others. With an eel section, we would lift the trap having put it in the previous night and it would be crammed with crays... and half of the eel section would still be pretty much intact. PERFECT!

✸ You can leave your trap in the water for anything between two to twelve hours. If you are leaving it overnight, secure the rope to something handy – a tree or a stick that you have dug in the ground will do. When you return, you should have heaps of crayfish in your trap!

EATING YOUR CATCH!

✸ You can eat all sizes of crayfish but the bigger ones – about 12cm from eye to tail – are best as there is more meat in the tail and claws. Put your catch in a bucket of fresh water for 24-48 hours as this 'purges' their system. When you have done that, simply place them straight in a large pan of boiling salted water for 4-5 minutes to kill and cook them. The shells will turn a bright red/orange – the same colour as a cooked lobster – when they are ready. Then you simply smash the claw with a small hammer or whatever you have that will do the job, twist off the tails and remove the meat from the shell. Expect a

mouthful from each claw and maybe two from the tail on good sized specimens. And don't forget to remove the 'gut', a black line that runs centrally down the tail. You don't want to eat that.

✸ Serve the meat in sandwiches together with some home-made mayo (see page 38 for our recipe), on their own with a squeeze of lemon juice and black pepper, in a salad, or with a tomato sauce to make a delicious spaghetti supper.

FISH IN FOIL

ONE OF THE SIMPLEST WAYS of cooking fish is to bake it in a foil parcel with some choice ingredients – and this method works fantastically well with trout and salmon. All you need to do in terms of preparing the fish is to gut it and, if it is a scaly fish, descale it (see pages 122 -123 for how to do this). Then take a length of foil at least twice as long as the fish and lay the fish on it. You can then stuff the fish with your chosen ingredients before folding the foil in half to cover it. The edges of the foil should then be rolled over and folded to create a seal. Just before you seal your parcel, make sure you have added a liquid that will create steam – this can be butter, water or wine. Make sure your parcel is properly sealed, as the moisture needs to stay inside to prevent the fish from becoming dry. Preheat your oven to 180°C, and then put the whole sealed parcel on a baking tray or rack and place in the oven.

We usually cook our fish parcels for 20-30 minutes, depending on the size of the fish. To check if it is cooked, make a small incision in the foil and pull away at the flesh of the fish with a knife or fork. If the flesh comes away from the bones cleanly, then it is ready. Remove from the foil and serve with all the delicious cooking juices.

Our favourite fresh fish foil combinations are below. (You can use these combinations of ingredients on fillets too if you prefer, adjusting the cooking time accordingly. I would suggest 15-20 minutes should be about right for a fillet.)

THE OLD CLASSIC

This combination is hard to beat when used with trout or bass. Squeeze some lemon juice over the fish and sandwich some lemon slices into the belly cavity, and season with rock salt and freshly ground black pepper.

Put a couple of bay leaves on the skin of the fish before sprinkling with thyme. Fold up the edges of the foil and just before you seal the last bit, pour in a good glug of white wine. Seal it up and bake in the oven.

Serve with some crunchy green beans and boiled potatoes. The buttery juice can be poured over the potatoes to round off a delicious seafood feast.

[PER FISH]

1 LEMON
4 BAY LEAVES
SPRIG OF THYME
½ CUP OF WHITE WINE

SPICE IS NICE

This involves a bit of spice and is best suited to mullet or sea bass.

Cut the lemongrass into 3cm long sections before crushing them to release the lovely lemony smell. Put this in the cavity of the fish along with the crushed cloves of garlic and sliced ginger.

Coarsely chop the chilli (taking great care not to rub your eyes afterwards) and sprinkle over the fish. Make a parcel, remembering to pour in the white wine last, and cook for 20-30 minutes at 180°C.

Serve with some stir-fried pak choi or chinese cabbage.

[PER FISH]

1 STALK OF LEMONGRASS
1 LIME
1 FINGER OF GINGER
4 CLOVES OF GARLIC
1-2 BIRDSEYE CHILLIES
 (DEPENDING ON HOW
 HOT YOU WANT IT)
½ CUP OF WHITE WINE

EXTRA PEP FOR POLLOCK

Pollock can be quite bland sometimes but if seasoned properly it is delicious. The intense flavours and colour from the chorizo will give it a hefty culinary kick and transform it Into a meal worthy of kings. As pollock is a pretty big fish, it is better to use fillets for this recipe, rather than the whole fish, but the same principles apply.

Pour a good drizzle of olive oil onto the foil and lay a fillet of pollock on top. Then spread the chorizo slices, bell pepper slices and bay leaf over the top of the fillet.

Splash a bit of water or wine over the whole lot before sealing up the parcel and baking for 15-20 mins at 180°C (again, a slightly shorter cooking time for a fillet required).

Serve with some lovely, fresh steamed vegetables.

[PER FISH]

1 SMALL CHORIZO SAUSAGE
 (AROUND 60G) SLICED
 INTO SMALL CUBES
1 BAY LEAF
1 TABLESPOON OF OLIVE OIL
2 BELL PEPPERS THINLY SLICED

MAYONNAISE

WHEN I WAS A CHILD, being dragged around a museum made me want to cry. But, there was one museum trip that captured my imagination, avoiding the stereotype of being unutterably dull and that was a trip to the Majorcan Mayonnaise Museum. Yes, say those three words again slowly: Majorcan Mayonnaise Museum. Here I learnt all there is to know about the eggy, oily goodness that comes in a jar of mayo. Thought to originally have come from Mahon in Majorca, mayonnaise, as it became known by the French, is an emulsification of egg yolks and olive oil.

Mayonnaise makes Trevor weak at the knees and he probably eats a kilo or so a week. This can become expensive and to cut our costs, we decided to make it ourselves. Turns out it is just oil and eggs. Try it, it really is very easy and tastes eight times better than any stuff you buy in the shops. Just remember to take your time. Mayonnaise is made from a forced mix of oil and water (from the egg yolks). Clearly these things don't usually associate with each other, which means that if the mixing is done wrong, the mayonnaise can separate or 'split'. This looks and tastes nasty and so is best avoided. The oil and egg yolks must be carefully forced to play with each other, which requires a fork and plenty of elbow grease.

As well as being delicious with pretty much anything, mayonnaise is the base for some other wicked sauces like tartar sauce, thousand island and ranch dressing to name a few. If you're anywhere near Trevor, though, don't let him see you using anything but the pure stuff; it upsets him.

Put the yolks in a bowl with the mustard powder and beat well with a fork. Add the oil as slowly as is humanly possible, whisking all of the time. Too quick and it will split. NOTE - You cannot go too slowly at this point!

After you've added about half the oil, mix in the vinegar and lemon juice, again whisking all the time. Continue to add the remainder of the oil, until it looks and tastes yummy. 300ml is a guide but will depend on the size of your eggs. Your mayonnaise will be much yellower than shop-bought stuff and once made, it will store for 3 or 4 days in the fridge. The shop stuff has preservatives that enable it to last longer.

(WILL MAKE ROUGHLY 250ML OF MAYONNAISE)

2 LARGE EGG YOLKS
1 CUP (300ML ISH) OLIVE OIL
1 TBSP WHITE WINE VINEGAR
1 TSPN ENGLISH MUSTARD POWDER
1 SQUEEZE OF A LEMON

SWIMMING OUTSIDE
AKA WILD SWIMMING

(It's free but it's cold. Brrr)

OTHER THAN JUMPING up and down on the spot or crawling, swimming is probably the first physical activity that any of us do as children. I certainly remember my mum taking me to the local swimming pool in Dartford to get my 10-metre swimming proficiency badge. However, the film *Jaws* slightly ruined my enjoyment of swimming for a while, until I realised that sharks in the UK weren't big enough to eat me and that Highdown swimming pool was an unlikely hideaway for a Great White – even in the deep end. I hear the chlorine stings their eyes.

But a good wild swim is something that involves more than just a session in the swimming pool. The mission to get to the secret spot, the anticipation of bathing in the coldest, freshest water, plus the view when you get there, all come together to make wild swimming something truly exceptional. (Not to mention its restorative effects on the worst of self-induced 'morning afters'.) I also think there's something deep within us that yearns to go underwater and be in the sea. There is some evidence to suggest that we humans, at some point in our evolutionary history, spent a good deal of time by and in the sea. Our lack of hair, downward pointing noses and the slight webbing between our fingers and toes, in comparison to most primates, certainly all point to a natural affinity with swimming and the water. And i am convinced that swimming wild, in the sea or in a lake or river, is something that links us with our long forgotten past.

One of my favourite wild swims is on the River Dart in Devon, as it flows through the Dartmoor National Park, near Hockinston Tor. The walk from the car park to 'Sharrah' pool, as it's known, takes about 45 minutes which weeds out all of those not up for a bit of a trek to have a fine swim. The pool is deep and has some excellent jumping and diving spots at either side. At the 'up stream' end are a series of tame, bubbling rapids which propel you, feet first, though the upper reaches of the pool, so you can float happily on your back, looking up through the dappled trees to the blue sky above; a pretty magical place. Top it off with an ice cream for a memorable day.

There are several books, websites and even societies that dedicate themselves wholly to the pursuit of wild swimming and we advocate all of them wholeheartedly, so just have a browse on the internet (**www.outdoorswimmingsociety.com** is one we particularly recommend). These websites will help you to find the perfect spot for a wild swim near you and, believe us, that may not be as far as you think.

The River Race

The inaugural Three Hungry Boys River Race took place when we were filming our first series in Scotland. We'd just finished clearing weed out of a fishing lake late one afternoon, which we were doing in return for a meal and some fly fishing lessons. Heading home, still wearing our drysuits, which are incredibly buoyant, we crossed a fast-flowing river, swelling with the rain that was bucketing down. The gamekeeper we were with knew the river well and said it would be safe to float down, and that there was a handy bridge further down river that could act as the finish line. We needed no further encouragement and all three of us got to work, blowing air into our suits to make them more buoyant, ready for the race.

We took our positions holding onto rocks to keep ourselves in place and then, on the count of three, we were off. The combination of a strong current and our buoyant suits made for an exciting first few minutes – we quickly gathered speed and were sailing down the river when suddenly there was a howl from Thom up front. It seemed that although the river was filling up with rain, it wasn't quite full enough to protect us from the larger rocks that were partially submerged. Thom had found one of these rocks with his bum – this was bad for him but good for Tim and I, as we were able to avoid where he got caught, and navigate our way to deeper water.

So there we were, Tim and I, neck and neck. And I realised this was an excellent opportunity to take the lead by pushing Tim into a bush that was growing over the bank. As we got closer I moved into position and when the bush came up I made my move, but sadly Tim had had exactly the same idea, and as we thrashed about trying to scupper each other's plans, Thom flew past us.

The finish line was around a bend in the river and there was only one course of action left for me. A pebbly, sloping beach had come into view. By running up the slope, I thought I could cut out the final bend, jump back in the river and conceivably win the race. As I was in last position, I had nothing to lose, so I got up and ran across the pebbled strip. I thought Thom and Tim would both be too distracted to notice but, alas, that wasn't the case, and as soon as I jumped back into the river, I heard shouts of outrage from behind me. They both managed to catch up with me on the home straight and we passed under the bridge together in a bundle. Luckily for them, I was slightly in the lead because just after the bridge there was a large metal bar just above the river bed that I crashed into. As I limped out of the river, the gamekeeper caught up with us: 'Might want to watch out for that metal bar under the bridge,' he said helpfully.

I guess the saying that cheats never prosper is true!

THERE ARE MANY WAYS TO SKIN A CAT - AND CATCH A FISH...

MAN'S OBSESSION WITH CATCHING and eating fish has produced no end of interesting methods to do so. And although 'fishing' is now generally deemed to involve the use of a rod and line, there are a few other intriguing ways to get your catch, should you a) be in the wilderness without a rod and with a rumbling stomach, b) wish to travel the globe in search of satisfying a fishing obsession that has taken over your life (like Thom) or c) feel the need to possess knowledge that can empty a room full of people in seconds (Thom again).

So, here are six methods of catching a fish, minus a rod, followed by our top six fishing adventures from around the globe which, if you manage to succeed at all 12, we truly believe will allow you to die happy.

CATCHING A FISH, MINUS A ROD

1. Okie noodling

Originating in Oklahoma (hence the Okie name), noodling is the act of catching catfish with your bare hands. It involves finding deep holes in the riverbank, putting your hands in and wiggling your fingers around like bait until the catfish bite! You then grab on and wrestle them out of their holes! Don't worry, though, their teeth are small and more like rough sandpaper so you won't lose your arm!

2. Catching eels on wool

An old method used by commercial eel catchers but which has now died out. The method involves creating a large birds-nest tangle of garden worms threaded onto wool. The eels come for the worms, but get their velcro-like teeth caught on the wool fibres, allowing the angler to pull the bait up with the eels attached. It is also known as quodding, babbing or snigging.

3. Trout tickling in North America

Rainbow trout, introduced and now very common in the UK, originated in North America. This is also where 'trout tickling' was born and is the act of reaching into undercut banks of the river and gently stroking the trout's belly, until it reaches a state of sleepiness and can be grasped with bare hands and pulled on to dry land.

4. Spearfishing

This involves freediving to hunt for fish underwater. You have to be able to find and spear your fish in one single breath. When successful, you will get a tremendous feeling and will have really earned your supper. You'll need to be well-fed when you do it though, as all that swimming and diving is hungry work. (See my section on spearfishing, on page 94 for more details.)

5. Handlining from a canoe

Do it like the tribes do. Cut down a huge tree, use half the timber for building a house and hollow out the other half to make your own canoe. Now get a length of line on a large spool, tie a hook on the end with some bait, and hope you hook yourself a tuna.

6. Flounder trampling

Each year in the small Scottish village of Palnackie, competitors roll their trouser legs up and wade into the River Urr in the hope of treading on, and then grabbing hold of, flounder living in the mud. Sounds odd to me, but also like great fun, and seeing as the winner gets three bottles of whisky (plus cash and a trophy, much less important than the whisky), it has to be worth a go if you're in Scotland in the summer.

AND NOW OUR SIX FISHING TRIPS TO DIE FOR:

1. The Marlin World Cup, Mauritius

Deserves the top spot hands down, these creatures are totally amazing. The three species of marlin are: blue (up to 1402lb), black (the world record for the largest is a massive 1560lb) or striped (the most beautiful, but smaller, with a world record of 494lb). After hooking them, the fight can last several hours and make you feel like you're trying to wind a train in.

2. Catfish in the River Ebro, Spain

Wels, aka European Catfish, grow to over 200lb and 7ft plus in length. These monsters give one hell of a fight, and, although a freshwater fish, you will definitely need strong sea fishing tackle to reel them in.

3. Salmon fishing in Scotland

Absolutely legendary; people travel from all over the world and can pay extortionate prices to get a permit for the best stretches of river. They do get big too, up to 64lb – a record that has stood since 1922, when Miss Georgina Ballantine pulled in her monster, making her one of the most famous female anglers of all time.

4. Bonefish on the Florida flats

Saltwater fly fishing in very shallow water. When you hook your bonefish, beware; they are renowned for stripping up to 100 metres of line on their first 'run' and you might not have enough! Exhilarating stuff.

5. Cod fishing in Norway

In this country, catching a cod is a pretty special thing. In Norway, they catch monsters of 25-40lb on every fishing trip. Add this to the fact that in the summer (June–August), there is daylight almost around the clock, and in the winter (October–February), the country is practically in total darkness, a trip to this unusual country will be one to remember.

6. Mahseer fishing in Southern India

Fishing in the rapids of the River Cauvery for these wild giants using lumps of soap, yes soap, for bait. And when you hook one? You have to get into a handmade boat that resembles a large wicker basket and follow the fish downstream, if you want any chance of landing him. It's kind of like fishing and whitewater rafting all at the same time!

2. ROCKS

COASTAL WALKS

THE COASTAL PATH runs, as you would expect, along the coast, although calling it a path doesn't really do it justice. When I think of a path I think of a couple of flagstones down to the shed or a maybe a nice mosaic-tiled walkway from the conservatory to the compost. These images are very much at odds with the reality of a coastal path, which can embrace a huge range of different terrains, from towering cliffs and pristine white beaches to lunar landscapes and of course the obligatory seaside amusement arcade. We're most familiar with the coastal path of the South-West from our university days but wherever you are in the UK, you'll never be too far from a stunning walk by the sea.

Some of the walks on the coastal path are little more than gentle strolls where the most you'll have to think about is where to find an ice cream, while others are rugged hikes where you'll be worrying about your shins snapping in half, so make sure that you have the right equipment for the job. A good sturdy pair of walking shoes, an ordnance survey map of the area and enough food and water for the day are a good start.

A good resource to get you started in the South-West is **http://www. southwestcoastpath.com**. You can plan routes and find out more about the areas from the website. I walked a part of the coastal path from Padstow to Land's End last year and was amazed by how beautiful and diverse our coastline is. Along the way, I took in endless white beaches, and the sea was never out of our sight, at times a deep turquoise, at others so clear that you could see shoals of fish beneath the water.

The path between Padstow and St Ives is a stunning stretch of 67 miles of relatively easy walks, the path is well marked and maps are available to guide you along the way. It's possible to walk this stretch with nothing more a packed lunch and sun lotion, and you can stay in one of the many B&Bs along the way. South of St Ives however the path gets tougher with loose rough surfaces and much steeper inclines. I would definitely recommend a good pair of walking shoes for this section. There is also a bus service that follows the path, so if it ever gets too much you can always hop on a bus to the next town for a well deserved drink.

RECOMMENDED DAY WALKS ON THE PADSTOW-LAND'S END COASTAL PATH:

Constantine Bay to Mawgan Porth – 8 miles – sandy beaches, dramatic cliffs.

Perranporth to St Agnes – 4 miles – cliff top walks with dramatic views.

Holywell to Perranporth – 3 miles – towering sand dunes, stunning white beaches. I think there may be a nudist area on the beach at the Holywell end, so you may have to shield your eyes.

SHELLFISH

THE TERM SHELLFISH is used to describe all the animals in the sea that have a hard, armour-plated exterior separating you from their delicious insides. Members of this club include swift, mobile, pinchy crabs, the well-protected and somewhat unusual limpets, whelks and winkles and, of course, the king of the gang, the elusive and very expensive lobster.

With some very basic equipment, all of these tasty morsels can be acquired from the rocky British coastline. However the amount of effort required to get them varies a lot, ranging from strolling down the beach to pick mussels, right through to pitting your wits against crafty lobsters deep below the surface of the sea, in a battle of psychological attrition.

SAFE EATING: A BIT OF SCIENCE

Before we go any further, we have to deal with some very important safety information. Shellfish sometimes get a bit of a bad name, as most people know someone who knows someone who once went to school with someone who shared an allotment with Tina and Tina's brother-in-law worked with a guy who once got really bad food poisoning from some dodgy mussels on the Costa Brava. The thing is this: shellfish generally belong in the sea and once out of the sea, they start to get a bit upset. So upset in fact that they die. Once anything is dead, it starts to decompose, opening the door for a wide variety of bacteria to multiply and set up shop. It is these bacteria that can make people sick. So the obvious solution is to make sure that your seafood is fresh and that you store it correctly before you eat it.

There is one other thing we need to talk about, and that concerns months with the letter 'R' in them. There is an old proverb that says you should only eat shellfish during months with an 'R' in them. Now I reckon that this dates back to a time well before the internet, scientists and research. What most probably happened is that people started to notice that during the hot summer months (months without an 'R' i.e. May, June, July, August), the shellfish they were

catching and eating were making people sick and therefore were best avoided. However, knowing what we know today, we can have a closer look and work out exactly what was going on.

Hot sunny weather in the summer months can sometimes result in large blooms of red algae, which, if eaten by filter feeders (mussels, barnacles, clams, oysters) can accumulate inside them and go on to poison their predators. But how does it accumulate within them? Well, these filter feeders are sedentary, which basically means that they sit on a rock and filter the water around them, hoovering up all the particles in the water and funnelling them directly into their guts. If you were a mussel, you'd basically sit on a rock with your mouth wide open, while sandwiches and burgers orbited around you and occasionally one landed in your mouth. The problem comes when there are other things in the water that aren't food. The mussels aren't able to distinguish between edible particles and non-edible particles. Imagine that along with the sandwiches and burgers floating around you, there are also used batteries and plastic bags. These non-edible particles also end up in their gut and have to work their way out of the mussels via the digestive tract.

OK, so shellfish are basically mindless

eating machines and whatever is around them eventually ends up inside them. But what is it about red algae that causes such problems? Algal bloom is made up of dinoflagellates (yup, hard word to pronounce) and it is these little guys that, when conditions are right, explode in huge numbers, covering the sea's surface for miles in the red bloom. If the dinoflagellates end up in, say, a mussel, they take a long time to work their way out of their system – by which time, that mussel might well be in your stomach. If eaten by humans, dinoflagellates can result in all kinds of nasty conditions that generally fall under the term PSP, or to give it its full name, Paralytic Shellfish Poisoning. These algal blooms usually occur in hot summer months so that too would explain where the 'month with an R' thing comes from. Algal blooms are thankfully rare, especially in the UK, and if they do occur, they are well documented by the media. However it is still always a good idea to check with locals and employ a good deal of common sense before eating mussels that you pick yourself.

So that concludes the safety talk. Is there anything else to know? Well, it is quite useful to bear in mind that in the summer months, bivalves (oysters, mussels, clams – so called

because they have two halves of a shell that enclose them) tend to rear their young. They change their body composition when they are doing this. They put all of their energy into their young and their bodies become thin and weak – and therefore not nice to eat. For another example of this, you should probably ask your parents how they felt after you were born. They will probably tell you how full of youth they were before you came along and how, ever since that day, they, and their wallets, have felt like a shadow of their former selves.

Another thing to watch out for with shellfish is pollution. As we have already discussed, filter feeders are none too picky about what ends up in their guts, so it's a good idea to have a proper look around wherever you are collecting shellfish. Basically, walk around and think to yourself, 'Would I feel comfortable swimming in this water?' The things to look out for are: harbours and marinas with dirty great boats, slicks of oil or fuel, sewage and industrial outlets, excessive amounts of plastic and refuse and nuclear facilities. If you see any of those, then it's probably best to avoid eating anything from that area.

ONCE YOU'VE LOCATED YOUR QUARRY

We'll go into the details of how best to catch each individual species later on, but for now we need to know the basics of what to do with our catch once we've got it. As your shellfish have just come out of the sea, you can imagine that they are none too pleased to see you. Most shellfish are able to survive out of water with the help of their exoskeleton but don't expect them to be thrilled about it. The best thing to do is to get them into a bucket with some seawater, and some seaweed for them to hide in. They will be more than happy like this for a day or so. But whatever you do, do not put them in a bucket of fresh water; this will kill them very, very quickly.

Prior to cooking, you should probably remove the worst of the sand, weed and other bits of flotsam and jetsam so that it doesn't end up on your plate, by basically scraping and scrubbing them as much as you can, followed by a good rinse. Some shellfish will need a bit more preparation before cooking but we'll cover that later.

Now that we've been through the basics, it's time to move on to the specifics: where to find and catch our delicious friends and more importantly how to cook and eat them…

MUSSELS

ON OUR TRIP TO SCOTLAND we had mixed success with mussels and funnily enough it was due to something we had never encountered on the south coast of England – and that was pearls. A lot of the mussels that we picked had pearls inside them which made them pretty much inedible, especially as we valued our teeth.

HOW TO 'CATCH' MUSSELS

The good news is that your quarry isn't going anywhere in a hurry nor will it fight back. Mussels are actually pretty rubbish at not getting caught; they rely on their hard shells and the fact that they live in the sea as their key defences. This makes it easy for us to track them down and to collect them. The bad news is that mussels can live in some very inaccessible places that you can only get to at certain times of the day, tide permitting.

Ideally, what you're looking for is a rocky shore in what is called the 'intertidal zone'. These are the bits of the beach that are underwater at high tide and exposed at low tide. The idea is that you wait for a falling tide and as the rocks become exposed you trundle over to where the mussels are, fill your bucket or bag with your goodies once you've pulled them from the rocks, and mosey back home when the tide comes back in. In practice what usually happens is that you get the tide wrong and end up clambering all over the rocks, desperately trying to find a route back to shore! This is the wrong way to do it. It is much easier and safer to check the times of the tide and work around that.

When it comes to actually catching the mussels, it is time to roll up your sleeves and get stuck in. Mussels tend to grow in clumps attached by what is known as a 'byssus' or 'beard' to the rock. This beard is quite tough and elastic and pulling it off can take quite a bit of effort. There will also be other things attached to the mussel like barnacles, whelks and seaweed. Discard what you can on the beach and the rest can be removed when you clean them properly at home. You'll want to pick mussels that are a good size to make them worth eating; about the same size as your thumb is a good guide, unless you have really small thumbs. As always, when foraging take only as much as you need and try to be selective when you pick. Don't wipe out an entire area as it will take a long time to recover. It's much better to thin out a larger area.

The barnacles on the shell can be very sharp so take care when pulling them off the rocks, you may want to bring a pair of gardening gloves if you have soft, sensitive skin.

Once you have a good couple of handfuls per person, it is time to return home with your spoils and enjoy what will most probably be the best meal, with the freshest mussels you've ever had. One thing to be very wary of is how you store mussels. While they can survive out of water, they don't really like it. The tide comes in and out twice a day, so they are usually not out of water for all that long. So once you have picked your mussels, get home as soon as possible. You certainly don't want to pick them in the morning and leave them in the sun all day. They'll die, causing their digestive enzymes to start leaking into their body, which ruins their flavour.

MOULES MARINIÈRE

MOST OF THE WORK with mussels goes into preparing them for the pot and after that, it is all plain sailing. This is a basic recipe, which can be elaborated on with extra ingredients but all you really need are the mussels, a couple of vegetables, and maybe a splash of wine.

THE OLD CLASSIC

[SERVES 4]

1KG MUSSELS
2 CARROTS
1 LEEK
2 CLOVES CHOPPED GARLIC
SPLASH OF WHITE WINE

The first step is to prepare the mussels. The best thing to do is collar someone who didn't help with collecting the mussels or the washing up last night. Explain that we live in a democratic society and that everyone needs to do their bit, give them a short, stout knife and tell them to get on with it. If everyone has magically disappeared, which is usually the case, then you need to sit yourself down and get ready to put some elbow grease in.

The mussels must be as clean as possible before you cook them, which means removing any tube worms (the white casings on the mussel shells), barnacles (little shells growing on the mussel shells that look like volcanoes) and other bits and pieces that aren't nice to eat. You also need to remove the 'byssus' or beard (mentioned earler) that the mussels use to hold on to the rocks. The way to do this is hold the beard in between your thumb and a table knife and pull it away. After 100 or so mussels, your hands might well be sore from all the scraping and pulling, so that's why it is a good idea to get some other people involved. Most importantly, if you come across any mussels that are cracked or open, these need to be discarded. If they close tight when you touch them they should be OK but if in doubt get rid of them. You should be left with a pan full of clean and closed mussels that will, in a matter of minutes, be in your belly.

All you need to do now is chop your vegetables and you're ready to start cooking. I like to put a splash of oil in the bottom of a large saucepan and fry the garlic and vegetables for a minute or two to get the flavours going. Once you can smell the garlic cooking add the mussels and splash of wine and put a lid on your pan. The moisture from the mussels, combined with the wine will be enough to steam them. You only need to cook them for around 5 minutes, any longer than this and they will become tough and chewy. It is very important that you discard any mussels that don't open after this stage; these are not good for eating.

Then simply spoon the mussels into bowls together with any juice from the bottom of the pan. To eat, pull the mussels out of their shells and mop up the juice with buttered brown bread. Or serve with some matchstick-thin *pommes frites* if you are feeling French.

For a hot, spicy Thai-style variation on this dish, you can add chopped fresh chilli, ginger and lemongrass to your pot of mussels.

COMMON LIMPET *(Patella vulgata)*

You can think of these guys as the cows of the rock pool. Found on rocks in the intertidal zone of rocky beaches, they happily graze on algae and often stay localised to one area. In fact, you can sometimes see where they have created depressions in the rock – places for them to shelter when the tide goes out. Limpets have a huge powerful foot that they use to clamp themselves to the rock when threatened. If you let them know you're coming, they will clamp down and nothing short of a rock will budge them. However, if you surprise them and give them a knock, they are easily removed.

Because the limpet foot is so strong it does make them somewhat tough to eat. We have been trying to find a recipe that makes them taste nice for years now. Apparently they were eaten a lot in the past – a fact proven by their shells having been found in middens (ancient piles of rubbish), so we can conclude that either a) we just haven't worked out how to eat them properly yet, or b) everything tasted horrible back then.

LIMPET AND MUSHROOM EN CROUTE

IF LIMPETS WERE A DELICIOUS FRUIT of the sea, you would have seen them being used as much as lobster or mussels or any other popular seafood. The fact that they're not tells you that they aren't delicious, but, they still can make an interesting dish. In our first series, we challenged Mull's best wild food chef, Tom Addy, to a limpet 'cook off'. We used an entirely foraged filling for our 'Limpet, wild mushroom and wild garlic ravioli' but unfortunately we lost to Tom's offering of a 'Bacon, cream (oh yes, and a little bit of limpet) strudel'. We've taken the best of the two recipes to make something that is both unusual wild food and actually quite nice – not always an easy thing to pull off!

Place limpets (in shells) in boiling water until flesh detaches from shell (about 2 minutes). Remove, and finely chop. (The limpet consists of a main muscle or 'foot' and a black body, both of which are edible, though the foot can be quite rubbery.)

Chop the mushrooms, spring onions, garlic cloves and wild garlic. Splash some olive oil into a frying pan and add the chopped ingredients along with the limpets. Cook for 4–5 minutes on medium heat.

While the filler mix is cooking, divide the puff pastry block into 6 equal portions and roll out to rectangles of 10 x 20cm.

Turn down the heat and add the double cream and seasoning to the filling mix. If the heat is too high it will split.

Gently simmer to thicken for 2–3 minutes. What you are looking for is a consistency that won't run when you spoon it on to the pastry.

Leaving a 1cm pastry-only edge, spoon the mixture onto one half of your rectangle parcels. Brush a small amount of milk round the edges to be stuck together, then fold over the empty half of the pastry making a neat parcel. Using the back of a fork, press firmly round the edges to seal the parcel and make it look a bit posh!

Place your parcels on a baking tray and pop in a pre-heated oven at 220°C until risen and golden brown (this should take about 10 minutes).

Great for lunch with a salad, or as a starter with a piccalilli (see our recipe for a great home-made piccalilli in the Urban chapter)

[FOR 6 PARCELS]

1 PACKET (500G) OF PUFF PASTRY
6–8 LARGE LIMPETS PER PARCEL
  (APPROX 40 TOTAL)
250G OF MUSHROOMS; button mushrooms (from the shop) are OK, but ideally forage your own. St George's, Field, Hedgehog or Chanterelle mushrooms would all work.
4 CLOVES OF GARLIC
1 HANDFUL OF WILD GARLIC
  LEAVES
8 SPRING ONIONS
200ML DOUBLE CREAM
SALT AND PEPPER TO SEASON

OPTIONAL EXTRAS:
SMOKY BACON OR PANCETTA,
SHAVED PARMESAN

HOW TO CATCH THE DELICIOUS RAZOR CLAM

These chaps are a real seaside treat to catch, not least because in most locations they are only available a few times during the year and with a very small window of opportunity. So grab them while you can – they are delicious! There are a few theories as to why they live in such limited zones of sandy shore, and there are also a few theories as to why salt makes them pop out of their holes so impressively. Personally, I think they like to live a quiet, sheltered life, although I can't be sure. What I do know is how to catch them. So read on to find where you should be looking and what you should be looking for. Each step is critical.

1.

First of all, you should be looking in one of two locations: either on sandy beaches (hopefully one where plenty of washed up razor clam shells are visible) when there is the largest of spring tides i.e. when the tide goes out as far as it is ever going to (in contrast to neap tides when the tide only goes in and out a little bit – for more explanation of this, see our Tides & Waves section in Sea Safety). This is because razor clams live in deeper water that is only exposed when the tide goes out pretty far, or in sandy bays which are very well sheltered nearly all of the time. (I think sheltered bays make the razor clam *feel* as if it is in deeper water.)

2.

Once you find one of these areas and the tides are favourable – i.e. out – wade out into the shallow water and look for small 'keyhole' shaped holes in the sand, which are created by the razor clams' two siphons being very close to each other. (The siphons are the holes which the clam breathes and feeds through.) In other species of clams, the two siphon holes will be further apart, and it is this smaller distance that can give us a clue as to what type of clam might be hiding under the sand before you dig it up. In bad weather, digging them up can be particularly difficult as the razor clams burrow very deep.

3.

Take a handful of salt (ordinary table salt is perfect) and, gripping it in your fist, place your hand underwater, and gently release the salt over the hole so some falls in.

4.

Now wait. This next bit will really test your patience. The first good sign is a small puff of sand, or some general movement round the 'keyhole'. Next the clam's head will slowly pop out, but you must still wait. You must wait, poised (still holding your breath, no doubt), until you can see at least 1-2 inches of shell emerge out of the sand, and at this point only, let the wrestling match begin!

5.

Grab the shell FIRMLY, on the hinge and opening sides of the shell (the strongest part), making sure you have a good grip. (Many a forager has lost his prize at this point; a lack of grip – a slip – and it's back down into the sand before you can say 'there goes my dinner'. Don't even bother digging and chasing him; these chaps burrow into the sand for a living, and are much quicker at it than you will ever be.) Hold on steadily (and you'll have to hold tight as they will really fight to get away) and pull with a constant pressure and within 20 seconds you should have your reward! As you extract your clam, the siphon may well fall off the top. This is a sacrificial offering by the clam, in the hope that the bird, crab or fish that is pulling at it will be satisfied with that, and the rest of the clam can retreat to safety. No such luck with us – it is the juicy 'foot' (that will be pulsating out of the bottom of the shell) that we are after.

6.

Now simply rinse any sand off your clam and cook, by steaming in a pan with some white wine, butter and herbs for a few minutes. Perfect – and it should be because you only get the chance twice a year!

SEAWEED

FIRST IMPRESSIONS on eating seaweed are generally that it is a bit rank. For the most part, those first impressions will remain uncorrected. Nevertheless, edible seaweeds literally cover our coastline and can bolster a forager's larder when times are hard, and provide an excellent source of the nutrients and minerals required in our diets. The Three Hungry Boys have eaten seaweed in a number of ways and very few (if any) have produced a delicious meal, but if you are stuck, and you need to bulk up, you could do worse...

Seaweeds have a distinctly salty flavour and a sometimes slimy texture – they can seem a tad unappealing when seen rotting at the top of a seashore, covered in flies. But although we don't eat algae too much here in the UK, it is a mega industry in other parts of the world, and, in the future, aquaculture (mass producing products from oceans/rivers etc for food, and even for fuel), is something we will most likely see more of on our shores.

As with all foraging, there are pitfalls to overcome. Yes, marine algae grow in abundance but you must always seek the landowner's permission before you forage on a privately owned beach. (See our section on Foraging and the Law, on page 151 for more information.) Also, you must take care to identify a good site to pick from and avoid a few inedible seaweeds. (There really are very few and they generally grow in pretty inaccessible places.) Seaweed is very susceptible to picking up toxic heavy metals in the water so you should take care not to forage from shorelines with heavy industrial connections. That said, E.U. legislation means pretty much all the coastline under their jurisdiction is now clean enough to pick seaweed from.

To make sure you are foraging sustainably, cut just above the holdfast, which holds the seaweed to the rock, and vary the area you pick from. Also, don't take all the seaweed you can see - a good rough guide is to leave a third of the algae behind so it has a chance to re-grow next year.

Some green seaweed can be eaten raw, and if you like regular trips to the toilet or doctors, go for it. However, even if you have picked it from a very clean area, I would suggest always cooking your seaweed before eating, just to make sure any nasty, stomach-gurgling bacteria are killed.

There are some species of seaweed that work well dried, and can provide a lovely, salty beer snack. Most seaweed contains a fair amount of iodine. Iodine is essential in your diet to aid the thyroid gland in regulating several bodily processes (controlling weight, growth, production of hormones and temperature for some) and is necessary for normal development of nervous and brain tissue in unborn children. A diet lacking in iodine can lead to obesity, sluggishness and even Iodine Deficiency Disease. So go for it... Seaweed is a great way of introducing this essential mineral into your diet, and it can even help weight loss! Eating way too much could cause other complications but you'd have to develop an unhealthy algae addiction for that to be the case.

So here's a guide to some of our favourite seaweeds.

Kelp *(Laminaria)*

These are the big boys. Kelp is what seals hide in to avoid being eaten by great white sharks. Kelp can grow a metre a day and reach up to 100m long. Kelp forests are beautiful to dive in and even in the UK we get our share of underwater kelp forests. It's not really eaten too often although it does contain a lot of energy. On our Scotland trip, we chopped it into little squares and deep-fried it in beef dripping. Unfortunately we did this in the dark, in a little caravan, and burnt a fair bit of it. Burning kelp gives off an aroma that not only burns the eyes but also leaves a long and lasting impression on your taste buds. If you are able to see, though, it's pretty simple to recreate yourself. Dry the kelp in the sun, chop into little squares and deep fry for 2 or 3 minutes. I'm sure Heston would do this three or four times then add a snail or two, but each to their own.

As kelp grows so fast, some have heralded it as a source of biofuel for the future, and I'm sure there's a fortune to be made in figuring out how to run a car on it.

Another great use for kelp is to burn it, which produces ash that contains an impure form of sodium carbonate; this can, among other things, be used to produce soap, which is quite useful if you're in the middle of nowhere and want to de-grease your pans.

Dulse *(Palmaria palmata)*

Dulse has a high protein content and pretty much all the nutrients you could want as a human being. It's great to add to things as a flavour and nutrient enhancer. Simply pick, air dry by pegging it to a clothes line, then add it to whatever you like. It's like a natural version of MSG in fast food, so it'll have people craving more of your cooking, and wondering what your secret ingredient is. Try it added to bread dough or to a meat dish like spaghetti bolognese.

Irish Moss/ Carrageen Moss
(Chondrus crispus)

Not all E numbers are bad for you. I didn't know that until my mum told me, long after I'd had it drummed into me that they were all terrible. E300, for example, is vitamin C and E407 is carrageenan, a large sugar-like starch that comes from boiling down *Chondrus crispus* in water. It can be used as a gelling or setting agent for puddings – not that we make many of them on our trips – or as a veggie replacement for gelatin, which comes from pigs.

Gutweed *(Ulva intestinalis)*

Literally looks like thin intestines when wet, and like stringy, green bogies when dry on a rock. Can be cleaned, rinsed, washed and rinsed again to remove the grit, eaten raw in a salad (if you're confident that you have sourced it from a clean spot) or deep-fried to produce oriental crispy seaweed. Trevor sometimes adds it to a potato rosti which makes it (mildly) edible – see recipe on page 68.

Laver *(Porphyra)*

You may or may not have heard of laver bread, a Welsh delicacy containing the boiled remnants of the seaweed laver. I'm not even sure the Welsh like it very much as it consists of boiling the hell out of the laver until it's a green pulp, changing the water many times over and mixing it with oats to make bread that you serve sometimes with bacon, sometimes with cockles, for breakfast. Now if I was really hungry I might gobble that up but normally I'd stick to my toast and marmite. The most common use of laver or *poryphyra* is to make Japanese nori, where the seaweed is spread out, dried and then used to wrap around sushi rice, creating a maki roll. It's definitely worth trying to make yourself rather than buying sheets of nori from the supermarket, mostly because you can then say you've made ALL of your sushi yourself!

Sea beet *(Beta vulgaris subsp. maritima)*

The seaside equivalent of spinach, only a little thicker in the leaf and to be honest, a lot better. Better why, better how? I hear you shout. Well, to start with, it is so common around the top of seashores that you can fill a black bag easily to the brim every time you go to the seaside. With the price of shop-bought salad starting at anything from £1.20 for a small bag, you could save yourself some serious cash, and food miles, in picking the wild option. And it is packed to the roof, I mean ab-so-lutely full, of vitamins. Even just looking at it makes you feel healthier. The thick, dark-green leaves hold their shape better than spinach during cooking, and sea beet doesn't do the disappearing trick once in the pan anywhere near as much as its daintier relative – highly recommended.

SEAWEED AND POTATO ROSTI

IF YOU ARE THINKING of using this recipe then it is safe to assume that things are not going well with your foraging. We experimented with these ingredients at the beginning of our Scotland trip when our larder was very empty and we had to improvise. The results were not great. To say this dish is an acquired taste really is an understatement. But if you have found yourself in the same position or you're just curious then please read on for a 'taste sensation'. The ingredients below are fairly rough, since you will most likely be cooking this with what is available.

A major issue with this recipe isn't so much the taste but the fact that no matter how hard you try, there will always be sand mixed in somewhere. So get ready to feel the crunch of sand between your teeth.

Right. Get yourself down to the shore's edge and snare yourself some gutweed (sea lettuce will also do – but do avoid the stringy tough seaweeds).

Take as much time as you can at this stage to rinse out the grit and sand. Every second spent doing this is worthwhile.

Peel and grate the potato. Set aside.

Using an equal amount of seaweed to grated potato, boil the seaweed in salted water in the largest pan you have for 1 minute. This softens the seaweed but also allows any sand or sand hoppers to separate and fall to the bottom.

Remove the seaweed using a slotted spoon and drain excess water.

Place grated potato, seaweed, flour, seasoning and extras (egg, chilli, paprika) into a bowl and thoroughly mix. Add extra flour if too wet until a firm patty can be formed.

Make your patty as thin as possible (1cm is ideal) and fry until golden brown on each side for a quick, crispy rosti. We had bartered some beef dripping from a fish and chip shop but vegetable oil is fine.

Serve with either sour cream or a spiced paprika homemade mayo (see our recipe for mayonnaise on page 38).

A 50/50 MIX OF GRATED POTATO AND SEAWEED

ENOUGH FLOUR (ABOUT A TABLESPOON PER LARGE POTATO) TO BIND THE MIXTURE

1 EGG PER 2 LARGE POTATOES

SALT AND PEPPER

OIL FOR FRYING

TRY A CHOPPED RED CHILLI OR SOME PAPRIKA FOR EXTRA FLAVOUR AND COLOUR

SEA BEET STIR FRY

THIS IS A RECIPE we often use when we have caught a white fish like sea bass or mullet. The fish is cooked very simply, wrapped in foil with some garlic or ginger, (see Fish in Foil on pages 36-37) and served with the sea beet stir fry. Sea beet is like a sturdy spinach with fleshy leaves that have a definite crunch, I like to combine them with pak choi and other Asian ingredients to make a quick and delicious post-beach dinner.

Roughly chop the sea beet and pak choi, finely chop the ginger, garlic and chilli. Heat some oil in the wok and then throw all the ingredients in for a couple of minutes.

I like to add a squeeze of lime juice, some fish sauce and light soy sauce for some added punch. Then just serve with the fish, and some rice or noodles if you are really hungry.

4 GOOD HANDFULS OF SEA BEET
2 PAK CHOI
ONE THUMB SIZED PIECE OF GINGER
2 CLOVES OF GARLIC
1-2 BIRDS EYE CHILLIS IF YOU LIKE SPICY FOOD
1 TBS COOKING OIL

HIDDEN POOLS

ALONG THE COAST, tucked away in hidden coves and out of sight from prying eyes, you'll sometimes be lucky enough to discover one of the coast's hidden rock pools. Very often these are large natural pools that have had the end nearest the sea sealed off with a concrete wall by locals. When the tide rises the seawater rushes in and when it falls, it leaves behind a pool full of crystal clear water, ready to be dived into. These pools usually have a healthy community of seaweed and fish living in them that also make a perfect safe place to snorkel, especially if you are a beginner. The sun's rays will heat the water in the pool nicely, so that even those of you who are put off by the sea's temperature can get in for a paddle. Just remember to wear something on your feet the first time you go in as there can be sharp rocks at the bottom. And definitely don't dive or jump in without checking to see how deep the pool is first.

Because the water in the pool is nice and still, the visibility is usually really good, so it's a great place to dangle a crab line to see how animals behave when you drop the bait. Next time you're at the beach, keep an eye out for a hidden pool and you might just be pleasantly surprised.

There was a man-made beach pool down the road from me when I lived in Bronte, in Sydney, Australia. I used to swim there as often as I could, sometimes after work when it was getting dark. When the tide was high enough, waves would break into the pool creating an effect like a washing machine. The turbulent water and fading light hid the ends of the pool so that it felt like you were in the sea, a truly magical experience!

WHEN WASHING MAKES YOU SMELL WORSE

On our trip to Scotland, we spent the majority of our time outdoors – we had Winnie, our VW camper van, for shelter but her facilities were pretty basic. She didn't have the luxuries of home like carpets or hot running water. This left us in a bit of pickle when it came to washing. After the first three days without a shower, the van had acquired a rather ripe aroma. We realised that we would have to make do with Mother Nature's washing facilities, so the sea became our bath. This is actually not as bad as it sounds; we got used to the cold after a while and it definitely left us feeling invigorated once we'd run back up the beach!

There was one occasion when it went horribly wrong, however, while we were on the island of Tiree. We'd had a fantastic day of surfing and because we'd been in the sea all day didn't really need another rinse, but Thom had found a big rock pool that he said we would love. Apparently it overlooked a stunning headland and we could use it like a sort of natural hot tub, as we watched the sun set. Tim and I took some convincing but soon we were all climbing over the rocks to get to the 'wonder pool'. When we arrived, we both had to admit that the view was spectacular and the rock pool itself was certainly big enough to hold all three of us. So far so good.

The pool looked pretty deep, so the three of us put our shorts on, grabbed our soap and jumped in. Being the tallest of the three I touched the bottom first, and I had the strange sensation not of hitting firm ground but rather of standing on what felt like layers and layers of jelly. When I got back to the surface the look on the faces of the other two told me that they had had the same experience. Just as I was about to say something, two almighty bubbles erupted from beneath us and the air was filled with the most appalling stench. It smelt like cabbage and Brussels sprouts mixed with egg mayonnaise and wet dog. In fact, imagine if a coach load of rugby players had eaten a breakfast of egg sandwiches, a lunch of cabbage soup and a dinner of potent curry. Then imagine that they had spent the day driving round in the hot sun with the windows closed so that the inevitable windy pops and bottom burps that emanated from their behinds had nowhere to escape to. Imagine the smell that would be left in the coach at the end of that trip and you would come close to the smell that came out of that rock pool.

Needless to say we got out pretty quickly with much finger pointing as to who the source of the smell was. Just as we were getting into a heated debate, the true culprit of the foul odour came to light. When we had jumped in, we had disturbed the pool's bottom, which had been covered in layer upon layer of rotting seaweed and been undisturbed for ages. Pieces of this seaweed now started to rise to the surface and the smell was getting steadily worse as more of it rose from the depths. Realising that our hot tub hopes had been permanently dashed we decided to cut our losses and head back to the van. (Although we had to go via the sea to wash off most of the smell.)

The moral of the story is that if Thom makes a suggestion about anything involving rock pools, sunsets or hot tubs, think twice before getting involved. You might just come away smelling worse than you did at the start.

3. SEA

HOW TO CATCH A MACKEREL

ALTHOUGH I HAVE heard of a challenge that involves catching a mackerel in every month of the year in the UK (apparently it's possible!), the summer months of June to September will, without doubt, give you your best chance to snare one.

During these months, the mackerel head into the shallower waters all round the UK to spawn and feed, often congregating in huge shoals that can stretch for hundreds of metres. Their ferocious appetite and seemingly small number of brain cells make them a relatively easy catch. Although I'm not completely certain that they have low IQs, I think it is a fair assumption to make, having caught some last year using a clothes label! Yes, you heard me correctly. In true Three Hungry Boys style, last year in Scotland, I fashioned a set of mackerel feathers (that are supposed to imitate the small fry that they feed on) by slicing the white washing label from Trevor's t-shirt and attaching strips of it to my hooks. I'll tell you how you can do the same on page 84.

An interesting fact about mackerel is that they must swim constantly in order to survive. They have no swim bladder (a fish's buoyancy aid which controls how deep it goes) so would sink if they stopped swimming. They also use a passive gill ventilation method to breathe, meaning they swim with their mouth open to allow water to pass over the gills. This constant swimming creates a firm flesh that means that they fight hard on the rod but are also one of the most delicious to eat.

THE METHOD

There are two ways to approach mackerel fishing – either by going out on a boat or by casting from the shore.

At almost any seaside town during the recommended months you should find a billboard or two advertising mackerel fishing trips. The boats usually go out for a couple of hours, and will supply all the bait and tackle required for you to catch yourself a mackerel. They are a great way to spend a fun, sunny afternoon with friends or family and are quite reasonable at around £10 per person – and you get to keep what you catch.

But although boat fishing provides a better chance of catching, I personally find catching my mackerel from the shore or pier incredibly rewarding. It is true that the success of this is largely dependent on the mackerel shoals being close to the shore, within casting distance but the atmosphere on a pier when a shoal is 'in', and everyone is crowding around, laughing and joking as they get in on the action, is fantastic. As always, we Three Hungry Boys recommend that in terms of conservation, you only catch as many as you need. There is no point in catching and killing just for the sake of it, so keep only as many as you will realistically use, and put the rest back alive.

IT IS WORTH BEARING IN MIND THAT:

✳ Mackerel freeze very well (already gutted, and while they're still fresh), and wrapping them individually in a plastic bag before freezing them ensures that they both freeze and thaw quickly, keeping the flesh top quality.

✳ In the past we've enjoyed a well-deserved pint in the pub after fishing, only to get chatting and persuade the landlord that some ultra fresh, line-caught mackerel (worth £5-6/lb; the best barterers know the value of their product) would be a top seller on his 'specials' board and that it may be worth a pint of local ale in exchange. 3HB motto? Don't ask, don't get!

✳ Check out our smoking. This, along with refrigeration, not only gives a great new flavour to your mackerel but preserves the fish for a little longer.

✳ Mackerel is a top sea-fishing bait for many species, and, in particular, works well for shark fishing (we get Blues, Porbeagles and Tope sharks in the UK) as rubby dubby – mashed and put in an onion sack, and hung over the side of the boat to draw in the sharks – so it may be worth taking extras back to a local fishing shop to see if they know any shark anglers who might need them... and then there's always the strange old lady with too many cats that need feeding.

HOW TO CATCH YOUR MACKEREL

1.

First, the kit: fishing for mackerel from the beach will require longer casts (of up to 100m to get into deeper water) and a specialist beach-casting set up, capable of casting the 5-ounce leads required. However, if you are fishing from a pier, the casting required is much shorter, as you are already out into deeper water, and a standard set up of a sturdy 10-12ft rod and reel loaded with 10-15lb line should be ample. This is the same equipment I recommend for catching pike, and will also work for catching bass and mullet. Despite having over 20 rods in my armoury, if I was forced to pick only one combination of rod and line for the rest of my fishing life, this would be it. It is just so versatile for both fresh and saltwater fishing.

2.

Next, the feathers. This is the most effective and popular way to catch a mackerel. They come in various colours but my favourite is a white feather, with silver coming second. The idea is to imitate the small fry that mackerel feed on, but, more importantly, you are also trying to catch the mackerel's eye. I feel white and silver feathers (especially in clear water on a sunny day, when the feathers will glint in the light) do this best. Pre-made feathers are simple to use, easy to find and cheap, at around £1.50 for a set with 4-6 hooks on. A small silver or gold spinner tied on the end of the line will also work well.

3.

A lead weight of 2-3 ounces will provide enough casting weight to comfortably reach 40-50 metres, using the rod mentioned above.

4.

The retrieve (i.e. the speed at which you reel in your line) can play a large part in a successful catch. If the mackerel are close to the surface, begin the retrieve as soon as your cast hits the water. Otherwise, counting a number of seconds after the lead lands before starting the retrieve and varying this count until you find the depth that the fish are swimming at is a useful tactic. Occasionally pausing during reeling in, and then sweeping the rod to twitch the feathers, can also prompt the fish to bite.

TOP TIP: pause or slow the retrieve when you feel a mackerel on one of the hooks. This gives the other fish in the shoal a chance to grab the remaining feathers, and getting a 'full house' (a fish on every hook) can really make your day.

HOW TO MAKE YOUR OWN MACKEREL FEATHERS

Improvisation is our middle name, and during our first TV series, we managed to blag our way on to a racing sail boat, and cook the crew moules marinière from some leftover mussels in exchange for a few beers, a packet of rice, six eggs and some good times. The boat had a rod with some old feathers on, but they had obviously seen good use (and a few fish no doubt) and by this point were not much more than a row of bare hooks tied to the line. I took the white washing label out of Trevor's t-shirt, cut it in to strips and put them on the line. With my first cast over the side of the boat, I had a 'full house' – a mackerel on each hook! It is hugely satisfying luring a fish on a set-up you have built yourself, not to mention that each homemade set will be about 1/3rd of the price of a shop-bought set, at around 50p. If you fancy giving it a go, here's how.

For a 4-hook set of feathers, cut 5 lengths of 40lb line, each 2ft long. Starting with line sections 1 and 2, tie a 3-turn water knot (see Knots section on page 136), leaving a 6-8 inch tag from the bottom of line 1. Repeat with lines 2 and 3, again leaving a 6-8inch tag from line 2. Repeat until you have 5 lines tied together and 4 tags of 6-8 inches long roughly 16-18 inches apart.

Attach the 4 hooks to the 4 tags of line using a blood knot (see Knots section). A blood knot usually uses 6 turns but as a 50lb line is quite thick, it might be better to use 5 turns or the knot may not tighten down properly.

Cut the washing labels into strips 8-10mm wide and 30mm long, hook once, thread a little round the bend then hook again, leaving a small section loose to flutter and attract the fish to bite.

WHAT YOU'LL NEED

40LB MONOFILAMENT LINE
3 OR 4 HOOKS, SIZE 2/0
WHITE CLOTHES WASHING LABELS
A KNIFE OR SCISSORS

Next, tie an overhand loop (again see Knots section for overhand loop) at each end of the line, top and bottom. This will be an excellent test of your fishing knots.

When it comes to fishing, tie your main line to the rod and reel to the top loop and a lead weight to the bottom loop.

Now, have a quick read of the 'how to catch a mackerel' article that will tell you where and when to go and what to do once you get there, and before you can say 'caught anything yet?' you'll have a bucket full of mackers ready for the best summer barbeque you've ever hosted.

HOT SMOKED MACKEREL

SMOKING MACKEREL is so easy even we can do it, and that means you can do it too. It does produce a lot of fishy smoke though, so it is something best done outside or, better still, on the beach.

A QUICK LIST OF NECESSARY EQUIPMENT

One sturdy pot with lid We have found that a good place to look for these is army surplus shops. It needs to be as deep as possible as you are going to be hanging fish in it. The pot we use is thick aluminium, about 30cm in depth and 50cm at its widest point, and is big enough to smoke about 5 fish at once.

Sawdust You can't use sawdust from pine or any wood with resin as it will taint the flavour of the smoked meat. You also shouldn't use sawdust from any wood that has been treated with chemicals. Oak sawdust is particularly good for smoking mackerel. You can get this from most coarse fishing shops or if you have a local furniture maker, you can ask them.

Wire/string This is to hang up the mackerel and so should be able to stand a bit of heat.

Oven gloves – or some sticks if you are feeling very rustic.

Brine This is where you can start experimenting; our favourite brine is made up of a cup of salt and half a cup of sugar, with some chilli flakes thrown in, and a litre of water. The idea is to make enough brine to cover your fish completely.

The first stage is to get some fish and prepare it. Follow our advice on gutting and filleting fish so you are left with nice, bone-free fillets. The fish then needs to go into your homemade brine for about 30mins. This locks in the flavour of the fish and adds the hint of salt and sweet.

The fish then needs to be air dried. The more moisture there is in the fish, the harder it is to smoke. To air dry it, you can make a clove hitch (see page 140), put the mackerel's tail inside, and pull tight. Hang that from anything outdoors, and leave it as long as necessary for it to become dry to the touch.

Now you need to prepare your pan. Sprinkle a light layer of sawdust over the bottom. Once dry, you can string the fish up in the pan. Run a wire across the pan, from one handle to the other, and then hang your mackerel by its clove hitch from the wire. Make sure it is well clear of the sawdust. Start off with a couple of mackerel, but add more when you have got your confidence.

Put the lid on your pot, and place on your fire or camping stove. The pan should be as airtight as possible to encourage the sawdust to smoulder and keep as much smoke in the pot as possible. You need quite a hot fire to get the sawdust to smoulder but once it's going keep an eye on it, to make sure the sawdust doesn't catch fire – though this has never happened in our experience.

About 20 minutes of hot smoking will give you golden brown fillets with a lovely, smoky flavour.

It's up to you to perfect the recipe of the brine and the amount of smoking but the general guidelines are the stronger the brine, the more intense the flavour. In terms of cooking, the more intense the heat the faster they will cook. Fish that are smoked and cooked very quickly will stay moist inside and should be eaten on the day or soon after. If you want to keep the fish for longer (if you are taking them on a trek for example) air dry them longer and then smoke them over a lower heat for a longer period, to remove as much moisture as possible.

Coasteering

My favorite country of all time is, without doubt, South Africa. It has everything a young adventurer could want – from wild open game parks and tropical sand dunes to cold water seas and warm coral reefs. But the one thing that really comes to mind when I think of this great country is its amazing coastline. In some ways it is not dissimilar to the coastal path round Devon and Cornwall, the only difference being that when you look out to sea in South Africa (at the right time of year), you have the chance to see some extraordinarily special things.

Coasteering (coast-eering) *n* – a physical activity that encompasses movement along the intertidal zone of a rocky coastline on foot or by swimming, without the aid of boats, surf boards or other craft. Activities usually include some or all of the following: hiking, running, climbing, bouldering, swimming, jumping/tombstoning, exploring/investigating, caving and foraging. Coasteering usually covers distances of 0.5–5 miles of coastline in often remote areas that cannot be accessed by means other than a boat. A similar activity known as Canyoning is the freshwater equivalent, exploring everything that a river or stream has to offer.

The all-time best coasteering I've ever done was on the Eastern Cape coastline. The rugged, remote and untouched terrain is not only beautiful but awesome fun. The trek I did covered about three miles and included rock climbing, steep hill walks, coves, caves and the most exhilarating cliff jumps into the sea. The guy I went with (who worked at the hostel I was staying at) had an intimate knowledge of the deep crevice where we jumped into the sea, and knew it rock for rock. He jumped in first, declaring that the water was much too deep for me to hit the bottom, although he did warn me about one small rock that jutted up from the seabed but didn't break the surface and would be invisible. He then proceeded to stand on that rock as I jumped, to make sure I avoided it. The cool, swirling water was a very welcome break after a hot and sweaty two-mile hike!

Anyway, on the last mile back to the hostel, when I thought my day couldn't get much better, I walked to the edge of a cliff to get a clearer view of the golden-red sun as it touched the horizon. There, almost directly below me – only 50 or 60 metres from the shore – in crystal clear water, was a huge humpback whale and her baby calf. I remember looking around in awe, wanting to share this stunning sight with someone. But my friend had gone on ahead, and I was completely alone. It felt like a dream, seeing something so amazing so close. I was sure the others back at the hostel would think I had made it up! The mother must have been almost 10m (33ft) long and the baby just a fraction of that size. They were heading down the coast to cooler waters to feed, after being up in the warmer, safer waters off Mozambique where the calf would have been born. That moment made me realise that if you head out to enjoy the great outdoors (and coasteering is the perfect way to do it) then sometimes, just sometimes, Mother Nature will reward you with an experience that will blow you away.

LOBSTER POTTING

'REAL' LOBSTER POTS ARE BIG, bulky, heavy, smelly, expensive things that unless you have a decent-sized boat are quite a mission just to get into the water. Not for you? Well we still love 'trying' (and occasionally succeeding) to catch lobsters, and have found a company (**http://www.yachtypots.com**) that sells collapsible, hard wearing pots for a reasonable price (around £20-30). They are perfect for the average beachgoer who is camping nearby, and if sea conditions are fairly calm, they are quite easy to position in the water just with a snorkel and mask.

TO CATCH YOUR LOBSTER, YOU WILL NEED:

1 collapsible 'multi-catch pot'

1 length of rope, which will attach your pot to your buoy, and is (plenty) long enough to accommodate the rise in tide, plus a minimum of 1/3rd again on top of that.

1 or 2 buoys for each pot/string. A couple of 4-pint milk cartons (yes, empty ones!) with the top glued on work a treat. You could paint them a nice bright colour if you fancy but they are usually quite visible just as they are. Keep your eyes peeled on the beach after a rough spell of weather, as commercial buoys sometimes wash ashore and these are, clearly, perfect for the job.

Weights to keep the lobster pots from moving. A few large rocks placed inside the pot usually help pin it to the bottom of the sea, but in extremely rough weather, don't expect the pots to be exactly where you first put them! Even the large, heavy commercial pots get moved around. That's why your long rope and visible buoys are important.

Snorkelling gear and, if the water is cold, a wetsuit.

TWO IMPORTANT TIPS FOR CATCHING LOBSTERS

You must consider both of these points or your chances of large-clawed bounty are limited:

1. Fishing baits

Until a short while ago, we used to use anything, from leftover bits of fish carcass and tins of tuna in oil to old meat bones, as bait for lobsters. But after doing a bit of research, it became clear that if you use specific bait for specific species, your chance of success is much greater. So the general rule of thumb is: use fresh fish bait for crabs and old fish bait for lobsters. The best way to make old bait is to 'salt dry' it, using any large plastic storage container (a Tupperware box would be ideal), filled with 4-6 inches of rock salt. Place any old fish heads/leftover fish (mackerel or herring are best) from a fishing trip, into the rock salt until they are fully covered. The salt will draw the moisture out and the bait will get old but won't rot. Try to salt your bait for a minimum of one month and it will be perfect for lobsters.

2. The location

Where you place your pots is key. You will not catch a lobster on a sandy seabed in the UK. This is a fact. It must be a rocky area with weed, preferably kelp. That is where lobsters live.

Early in the year (springtime) is the perfect time to catch lobsters as they are still close to the shore. At this time of year, simply wading out up to your waist at low tide to put a lobster pot in the water, and leaving it for a 24-hour soak will give you the chance of getting one. (It is best to leave your pot overnight, because that is when the lobos come out to feed.)

Before you put a pot down, though, make sure to check what the local rules are. Some areas allow a maximum of 6 pots per person before the potting is considered commercial, while others only allow pots to be put down at certain times of year; and still others require a licence for all potting (though it may be free of charge). And, in all places, there is something called a Minimum Landing Size. This means if you catch a lobster which is smaller than the stipulated size, you have to put it back in the water. It is incredibly important for sustainable stocks (and to avoid a hefty fine) that this limit is adhered to, so please, please put any undersize catches back. The size limit is generally any lobster with a carapace length of less than around 85-89mm: the length from the eyes to where the main 'head shell' finishes and the segmented tail begins. It is also necessary to put back any females that are nurturing eggs (they harbour these inside their tail flaps – look out for a mass of small dark balls).

METHOD

✴ To set the pots fishing, tie one end of your rope to the main frame of the lobster pot, using a bowline knot (see Knots section) and tie the other end securely to your buoy in a loop using the same knot.

✴ At very low tide, put your wet suit on if necessary, and snorkelling gear, and either walk or swim your pot out to the right area, rocky and weedy – not sandy. If the water is over chest height where you want to place it, you will have to drop it down and then dive under to place a few rocks (that should be scattered around on the sea bed) inside the pot to give it a bit of weight and stability.

✴ Leave it for 24 hours and return the next day at low tide again. Find your buoy floating on the surface and pull the rope in hopefully to discover a pot with one (or more!) lobsters inside.

PREPARING YOUR LOBSTER

✴ To humanely kill it, place your catch in the freezer for a couple of hours which will put it into a sleepy, numb state, and then plunge it straight into boiling water, for between 12 and 18 minutes, depending on size.

✴ Once cooked, remove from the water and allow to cool before removing the claws by twisting them off from the body. Then split the body and tail in half lengthways using a large heavy knife. You can then either remove the tail meat from the shell or keep it in the shell and cook it on the barbeque.

✴ The tail meat and claw meat are the best. (Remember to remove the thin black tract running down the length of the tail. This is the gut and shouldn't be eaten.) A good old-fashioned hammer and a pair of pliers to hold the claws steady while you smash the tail and claws will help to get the meat out.

✴ There's thermidor, bisque, and a few other classic recipes which you can find in any good shellfish cookbook, but for us, just grilled on the bbq with a bit of garlic and a melted butter dip really tops the list. Keep it simple and enjoy!

CATCHING FISH WITH RODS, HOW VERY LAST YEAR... HOW TO SPEAR FISH

SPEARFISHING IS A SUSTAINABLE, healthy, environmentally sound way of getting yourself a fish to eat. Some might say it is cruel or inhumane, but I challenge them to tell me where the leather of their shoes came from or how the chicken in their nuggets made it to their plate. With spearing, I know what I eat is fresh, because I've looked it in the eye.

Usually fish from the oceans arrives at our table via a large indiscriminate trawler net or a waste-producing fish farm. Fish are caught and kept according to a strict quota but unfortunately, most nets can't discriminate between the fish they want and those they don't! You will probably have seen Hugh Fearnley-Whittingstall's BAFTA-winning *Fish Fight* campaign, which aims to raise awareness about the horrendous over-fishing that goes on, and to reduce by-catch, the term used for when fish are thrown back in to the sea, dead, because it would be illegal for the fisherman to land them. How can we do our bit? Simple. Buy a wider range of fish to eat. Instead of the big three – tuna, salmon and cod – buy pouting and mackerel and whiting and conga and all the other delicious fish in our waters. Better still, let's go and catch them ourselves!

SAFETY FIRST

✳ Never spearfish on your own. It's just silly. Any mistake – a boat going over you, a tangle with a fishing line or cramp from swimming within an hour of eating (against the advice of our mothers) – and you could find yourself in a pickle more pickly than a cheese and pickle sandwich. So, find yourself a mate, but one you trust, who doesn't hold any grudges, for in all likelihood they will have a spear gun too.

✳ Don't load your spear gun until you are well into the water and away from others. I have seen many a gun misfire where the spear wasn't firmly connected to the shaft. From close range, a spear would easily shoot, if not straight through a person, then most of the way. Also, carrying spears across public beaches or car parks can get you some stern looks. Popping someone's tyres, or snagging a Range Rover won't earn you any friends, so be careful.

✳ The use of an SMB (Surface Marker Buoy) to show where you are diving is essential (see on page 99 for more information), as ideally you will be quite well camouflaged. You're not going to have much luck hunting fish in a neon yellow wetsuit – most spear fishermen opt for a specialist black or camouflaged suit. This makes you quite difficult to spot from a speeding boat or jet-ski and makes the buoy hugely important, signifying your whereabouts to anyone in the water.

THE LAW

It's very important to know where you stand with nice Mr Policeman when you're carrying a potentially lethal weapon across a beach covered with children, or through a car park where old people in cars like to look at the sea. Ninety-nine times out of a hundred, people will smile, nod and understand that you are a mighty warrior of the oceans about to save the world, one deep breath at a time. The odd person, however, may question your status as Poseidon and it's helpful to know where you stand. In the eyes of the law, spear guns are treated as potentially offensive weapons. It is illegal to spearfish in the UK in any body of water without a tide (i.e. rivers, lakes etc) but permitted in most tidal areas (estuaries, open oceans etc). Be careful, be polite and be sensible when holding your spear gun and you should be just fine and dandy.

It is also advisable to know that things look bigger underwater and there are legal guidelines (DEFRA's Minimum Landing Size) on the size of fish you can take home for tea. You are unlikely to catch or want to eat fish smaller than their recommendation but for your peace of mind, it's worth knowing what these guidelines are before you begin.

Finally, if you go on any forum about spearfishing, there will at some point inevitably be a discussion on whether spearing a fish underwater aided by scuba gear is illegal. Having trawled the UK legislation website for an actual law, I can't find one. It is, however, very much frowned upon. It's the equivalent of shooting a deer from a microlight with a machine gun or catching carp by dangling some highly charged wires in the water and catching what floats to the surface with a net. In short, it's not sport and even if you can, you probably just shouldn't. (But it is tempting when spearfishing in the depths of winter, when visibility is zilch and it's so cold that your fingers are numb.)

As a potentially lethal weapon, spear guns can only be sold to over 18s and must only be used underwater. I tried once on land and nearly lost a testicle. Nuff said.

WHAT YOU'LL NEED

Spearfishing is an ancient form of catching fish for supper and, pre-goggles, was done from a boat or a riverbank, with a long sharpened stick and a lot of patience. Modern spearfishing will normally happen underwater, with a snorkel and mask, fins (not 'flippers') and a metal spear that uses one or two pretty large elastic bands as a means of propulsion. You may also want to take a knife, a net bag, a clip for stringing up your quarry and a torch. It's a pretty intense (but not intensive) method of fishing and requires a fair amount of skill practice and dedication. It is definitely not cheaper than buying fish, or easier than catching them with a rod and line, even in the long run, but in my opinion is certainly more rewarding and definitely more fun.

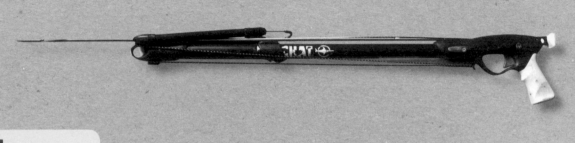

1. Spear Gun

There are many brands of spear gun and, as with many things, all have their merits and drawbacks. Whatever your budget, it is worth noting that an inexpensive spear gun may frustrate you. I know because I've been there. On holiday in Greece, I spent my meagre savings on a hand-held, air-powered pistol spear gun. I can't begin to tell you how disappointed I was when firing it underwater. A little anger still wells up inside when I think of the smiling Greek man who sold it to me, knowing that I was as likely to shoot a Hollywood blockbuster as I was a fish with it. The important things to consider when making your purchase are the length of gun, the type of catch and the quality of the rubbers. The spear's barrel length can increase from about 45cm to over a metre, in 10cm increments. We have quite a few at 3HB HQ and our favourite is probably a Beauchat 75cm, as the parts are easy to get and they're pretty reliable. As you get more experienced, you may wish to buy a bigger, more powerful gun but a 60 or 75cm one is a good starting point.

Some guns involve nothing more than a wire loop that is pulled over the catch in the spear, but the better, more expensive guns have a more intricate catch that will fit nicely and securely into place over the spear. The rubbers (the mechanisms used to propel the spear) come in different diameters and are either in a loop or fix into pre-fitted crew holes. Either is fine but the thicker the diameter, the better for power – and the harder to load.

2. Fins

There are two types of fin (NOT to be called 'flippers', which is the name of that dolphin from the 80s). Full foot fins are for use in warm waters and have no room for a sock or wetsuit bootie underneath. They're pretty unsuitable for long periods in the water in the UK, except maybe in the warmest waters in the autumn. Foot pocket/strap fins are more widely used in colder waters and for scuba diving. Apnea/free divers and some UK spear fishermen use really long fins for extra power and speed. The down side is a lack of manoeuvrability. Climbing in and out of rough, rocky water with hugely long (I'm talking up to 6 foot) fins isn't too much fun. Try on as many as you can to see which suit your swimming style.

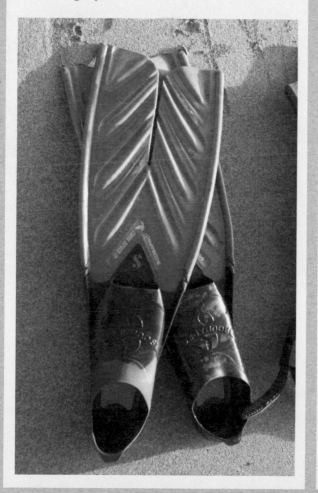

3. Snorkel and Mask

The only times I've ever experienced anything close to danger underwater have been when I'm stressed out because I have a leaky mask, or it doesn't fit properly. Stress is an absolute killer in scuba diving and snorkelling and so well-fitting, fully-functioning gear is essential. As such, I can't really recommend a mask to anyone except to say, make sure it fits really well. I personally use a Cressi Sub as it fits my face shape perfectly and I love the Italian styling. Thom wears a US Divers and Trev a Northern Diver. It really depends on what you feel comfortable in. Some key words to look out for when choosing a mask:

Low volume – this makes your mask easier to 'clear' underwater and sits closer to your eyes giving better peripheral vision.

Black/clear lens – black lenses let in less peripheral light, making some people feel claustrophobic; clear ones let in more light but allow the fish to see more of your – ie Trev's – milky white skin.

Framed/flat folding – flat folding masks are great as backups in a scuba kit but feel a bit flimsy for me for regular use. I would go for the sturdier, framed version every time.

4. Knife

Although I've never had to use mine, I always carry a knife when diving or snorkelling. It doesn't need to be massive but does need to be sharp enough to be useful in the unlikely event of your getting tangled in something nasty underwater. They're also exceptionally useful for dispatching and gutting fish before you leave the shore to avoid doing it later. Ideally get one with straps so you can strap it to your calf or thigh; if not for safety, then because it makes you feel like a baddy in a James Bond film.

5. Weight belt

We humans are nearly neutrally buoyant, enabling us merrily to swim up and down in water with no force pushing us upwards to swim against. The issue comes when we put on a wetsuit. The upward force of the suit's buoyancy makes getting down to the sea bed and staying there quite tough. The trick is to have just enough mass on your belt to allow you to descend on an exhaled breath, wearing all of your kit, and to stay afloat on a full lungful of air. It's a fine balancing act and one that takes a few goes at getting right. You need to know how much to use for your specific wetsuit and whether you are in fresh or salt water makes a big difference. Belts are handy to hang things off too; I attach my stringer for tying up dead fish (more on which to follow), a loop for a torch and an SMB reel.

6. Net bag

You may encounter other edible goodies when spearing – urchins, scallops, mussels, oysters, some seaweeds to name a few – and having somewhere to put them is a jolly good idea or you'll end up drowning yourself trying to carry them back to shore (I know from experience). I find the best way to keep it out of the way when not in use, is to roll it up and stick it up my trouser leg. Simple but effective.

7. Stringer or Fish Clip

Designed to keep the fish you catch safe until you get out, a stringer is a useful bit of kit. Essentially a big safety pin to hook the fish onto once you've shot them, it's the easiest way of carrying them. Obviously, there are not too many dangerous shark species in UK waters, but it is as well to know that you are a little more likely to be attacked when carrying several dead fish on your belt. No more likely than, say, winning the midweek lotto, but the risk is still there. I have seen a 6-foot Tope (a type of shark) take a mackerel from right under our noses, in the waters off Tiree, on the west coast of Scotland, so anything's possible. Just a warning!

8. SMB – Surface Marker Buoy and reel

Basically a solid or inflatable buoy that is attached to your spear gun, and follows you round, marking your position in the water.

Right, once you've got all that sorted, It's time to actually go spearfishing. The gear is very important but the technique is even more so and must be practised. There are some pretty big factors that can sway your chances of hitting fish either way. You may still go hungry yet.

WHERE TO GO AND WHAT TO DO WHEN YOU GET THERE

Where to go should be quite simple; where the fish are. Unfortunately, in practice, it may take you a while to find the best, most appropriate spots for a spear. Trev, Thom and I took a trip to Portland Bill in Dorset where we'd heard of monster shoals of bass and pollock swimming off the rocky reefs in clear water. We made a day trip there to find clear blue skies, crystal blue water and not a single fish worth shooting. Not one. Not even a wrasse.

In general, anywhere where there's food about should offer some sizeable fish. I always get excited when I see shoals of tiny silver sprats because you know that somewhere lurking nearby will be a bass or two, and certainly some pollock. In the UK, the species you're most likely to see will be mullet, bass, pollock and some flat fish. Flat fish like turbot or plaice, will normally be found around sandy-bottomed sea beds but you will be bored to tears looking for them as

they are very well camouflaged. You may also find the exceptionally tasty grey-lipped mullet feeding in the surf of sandy beaches. We have had the pleasure of introducing ourselves and our spears to great shoals of them on Cornish fishing trips. The elusive bass and larger pollock will be harder to catch, with numbers generally lower and having a more easily-spooked nature.

We have found that rocky gullies covered with weed forests of kelp have always been a good spot to spearfish, but internet forums can point you towards good sites near where you live.

The most important thing is to get to know a dive site well, and over the course of a whole year. Underwater habitats change with the seasons too so it's a must to find your site, and then dive it again and again, getting to know it intricately. You'll start bagging yourself some tea in no time.

1. Loading a spear gun

Always have the safety catch on when loading your spear gun and never have it pointed at anyone. Making sure the spear is correctly and securely seated in the trigger assembly, place the butt of the spear against your chest or waist and reach forward, grabbing the two long elastics, one in each hand. Pull back and hook the spear catch into the groove on the spear, making sure it's settled well. Secure the fishing line to the gun's line clip so as not to get into a tangle.

2. Spearing a fish

The actual art of spearing a fish is a lot more difficult than it sounds. You've got to hold your nerve, take aim and hope you haven't left the safety catch on, all whilst holding your breath. Diving down and concealing yourself among the weeds, swimming stealthily through rocky gullies and keeping low to sandy bottoms is all made much easier the better you are at doing this. On land, I can fairly comfortably hold my breath for over 3 minutes, as long as I haven't been running about. In the cold, finning hard against a current and with my adrenalin pumping, this is often brought down to less than a minute. The best way to improve this is to use a technique called 'cycle breathing'. Dive down in to the water for a short time, and then follow this with a roughly equal period on the surface. So a 20-second dive should be followed by 20 seconds spent on the surface. Then repeat. You shouldn't become too out of breath, and you should be able to repeat this a fair few times. This will tire you out less than struggling to do long stints underwater, and gulping for air at the surface. So, using a surface duck dive, head straight for the sea bottom, keeping an eye out for any fish around you. Once at a good depth (or the bottom), pick a path through some kelp if possible or very slowly move towards the place where fish have been spotted. Slow and steady movement plays a big part in not spooking any fish, so keep your fins strokes long and try not to jerk about. Your spear should be out in front, in your field of view.

3. Pulling the trigger

Remember when the moment comes, and you see a fish of the right size, i.e. worth shooting, that things look closer and bigger underwater. The blood will rush to your head and your adrenalin will make your heart feel like it's about to burst through your chest. Slowly take aim, slightly above the fish's head and gently squeeze the trigger.

Happy fishing

CATCHING CRABS

IF YOU ARE AFTER CRABS for dinner, you are going to have to have your wits about you. One lapse in concentration and you run the risk of feeling a vicious pinch. There are numerous species of crabs found on the UK shore line that you can eat but the kind you find in the supermarket is the edible crab or brown crab (*Cancer pagurus*). Edible crabs can grow to be pretty big; they have a reddish brown body and large powerful claws. The edge of their carapace (main shell) has a crinkled edge, much like a Cornish pasty, which seems to me to be its way of saying 'eat me'. The larger edible crabs are only really found in deep water so you'll have to use a pot to catch them. Again, as with different species of fish, and lobsters, a Minimum Landing Size applies to edible crabs if you want to eat them. This varies slightly from area to area in the UK but 160mm for males and 140mm for females is a safe guide.

WHAT YOU'LL NEED TO CATCH EDIBLE CRABS
To catch edible crabs you'll need one of the pots mentioned for lobster potting, together with all the associated kit and some bait. However the bait you should use differs from that for lobster. If you want to catch crabs, you'll need relatively fresh fish (1-2 days old).

METHOD

Take your pot out to deep water (a depth of 10m plus), bait the pot and leave it in the water for at least 24 hours (following the instructions from the Lobster potting section for how to place your pot). Hopefully when you pull it back up, you'll have lots of big crabs staring back at you. Remember to check their size and if you catch any females which are 'in berry', which means carrying eggs, you need to throw them back. Look at our photos to show the best way to pick up your crabs without getting a pinch!

There are two other kinds of crab that are 'edible', which are found in shallower waters than the edible/brown crabs. Velvet swimming crabs (*Necora puber*), are a delicacy in Spain where they are prized for the sweetness of their meat. They get their name from the short hairs that coat their body, giving it a 'velvety' feel. They are also extremely vicious.

You can also eat 'shore crabs' (*Carcinus meanas*), but they are very small and you can end up spending more time getting the meat out than actually eating it.

The best way to catch either of these types of crab is to tie a piece of meat or fish to a line and simply dangle it into a likely looking rock pool or off a harbour wall. You'll feel the line being tugged once a crab gets on to it and then as quickly and smoothly as possible pull it out of the water. Hopefully your crab will still be holding on.

HOW TO PREPARE YOUR CRAB

✳ Once you have caught a crab, it is important to keep it in a cool, damp place. What we usually do is get a bucket and put the crab in there and cover it with seaweed. This not only keeps the crab at the desired temperature but also keeps it calm, as it can't see our ugly mugs!

When you get home you should put your crab in the freezer for a couple of hours. As with a lobster, this will slow its metabolism down and put it in to a deep sleep, a kind of hibernation.

✳ When you are ready to cook it, you should put the crab on its back, and then get a screwdriver with a small point, or a skewer, and lift up the flap on its belly. Under the flap is a small opening. Push the tip of the screwdriver or skewer into that opening hard, as far as it goes and wiggle it back and forth. This kills the crab very quickly and as it has already been in the freezer is pretty humane.

Cook your crab immediately after this. Don't leave it sitting around as it will start to go off as soon as it is dead. So drop your crab into a large pan of boiling water: 20 minutes for a crab up to 2lbs, and add five minutes per lb over that.

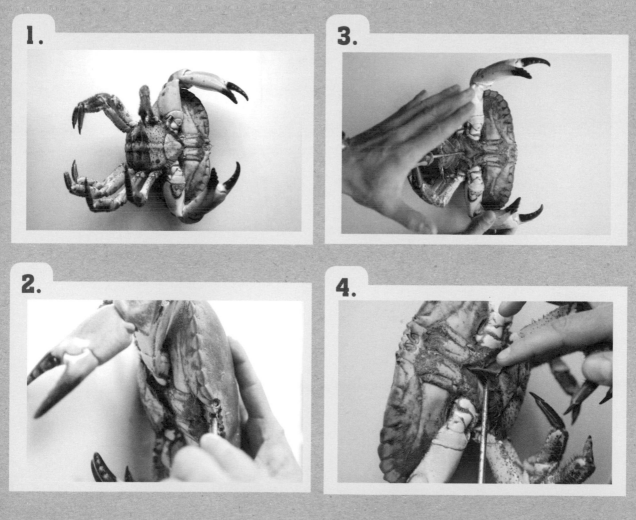

1.

2.

3.

4.

DRESSING CRAB

You will need some bowls for the crabmeat once extracted, a rolling pin, and a thin pick, or narrow spoon. Take your crab, and lay it on its back. Twist and pull the two main claws from the body. Next pull the legs off (1). Then, with four fingers of each hand, hold the main shell, and, with your thumbs underneath the large triangular flap at the back, push forward, and the triangle flap and innards will come out in one piece (2 & 3). From that main section you have removed, you will see hanging from each side of the body several grey, slightly pointed soft triangles between an inch and two inches long (4). These are called 'dead man's fingers' and are the lungs of the crab. They are not to be eaten – make very sure not to get them mixed in with the crabmeat (5). Also, with your pick, remove any meat from the holes on the main body that are now exposed (where the legs were).

Now, on a sturdy surface, bash the large claws with a rolling pin (a small hammer will work too) and this will expose the meat within; the best in the crab (6). Make sure also to get any meat out of the eight legs you have pulled off (7) – break the legs at the joints to expose the meat, and then using your pick or spoon, push any other meat out that is hard to reach.

Brown meat will be found in the middle section – most people like to keep the white meat and brown meat separate, as the brown is a stronger taste – and if you don't like to eat it on its own, it can be a great addition to other things like soups.

Eat the meat straight away or rinse out the main shell and spoon the white meat into one half and brown meat in the other (8), and serve with some lemon juice and salt and pepper.

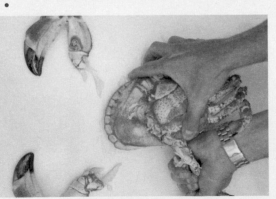

1.

2.

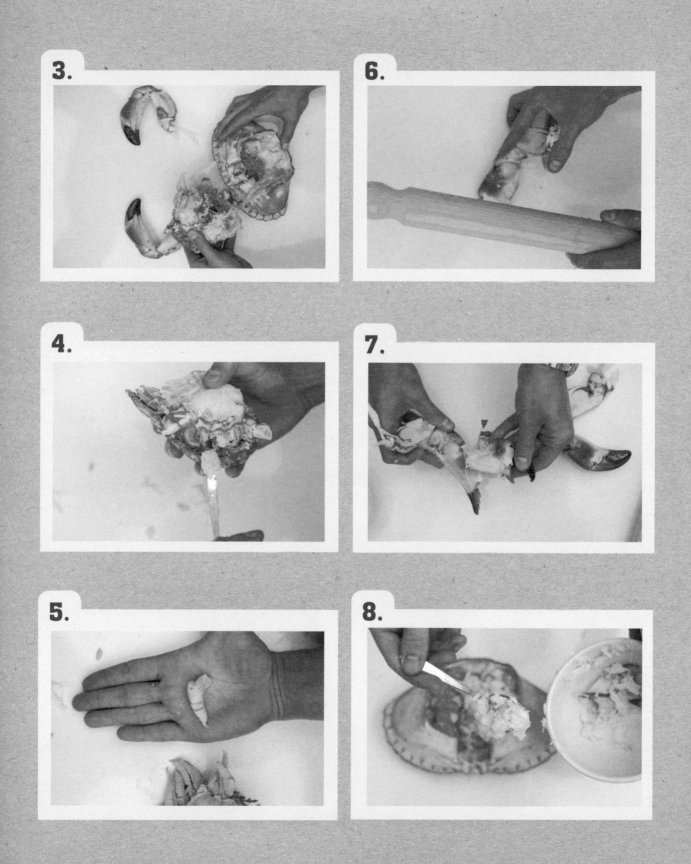

OYSTERS

SCALLOPS AND OYSTERS can be more effort to locate than mussels and whelks, and you need a good man or a lot of research to find an oyster bed or scallop patch. Their location (as with a good mushroom patch) tends to be a highly guarded secret. I found one of the oyster beds I harvest by being pretty canny. I discovered that some local schoolchildren had done a project on the oysters in the area and had put it on the internet with the precise location.

There are two species of oyster you are likely to come across in the UK. One is the Native Oyster, fairly small and round in shape, which is a protected species so must be left where it is. The other is the Pacific Oyster – a farmed species that has run wild. My tip is to find an oyster farm and then look on the shore in the nearby area for some escapees! You will need a really tough diving knife to weasel them off the rocks, a bag to put them in and a small rock to bash the knife with – these oysters are stuck on hard!

HOW TO SHUCK AN OYSTER

Shucking an oyster is quite a trick. On shucking my last batch of 12 wild oysters I broke three knives and a pair of scissors, so it may be worth getting yourself a dedicated shucking knife if you're going to be eating them often. Lay the oyster on its 'back' with the flat shell on the top and the spoony, curved shell underneath (1). Protect your hand with a tea towel in case the knife slips (2). Hold the oyster with the point towards you and slide the knife into the hinge at the end (3 & 4). Once inside, you should be able to open it completely with a satisfying pop, revealing the bounty inside. Now that it is open, simply slide your knife under the oyster meat to cut it from the shell (5–7). If you really like oysters then you might like to just slide it out of the shell and straight into your mouth. Otherwise a squeeze of fresh lemon and a few drops of Tabasco are an easy and delicious addition.

1.

2.

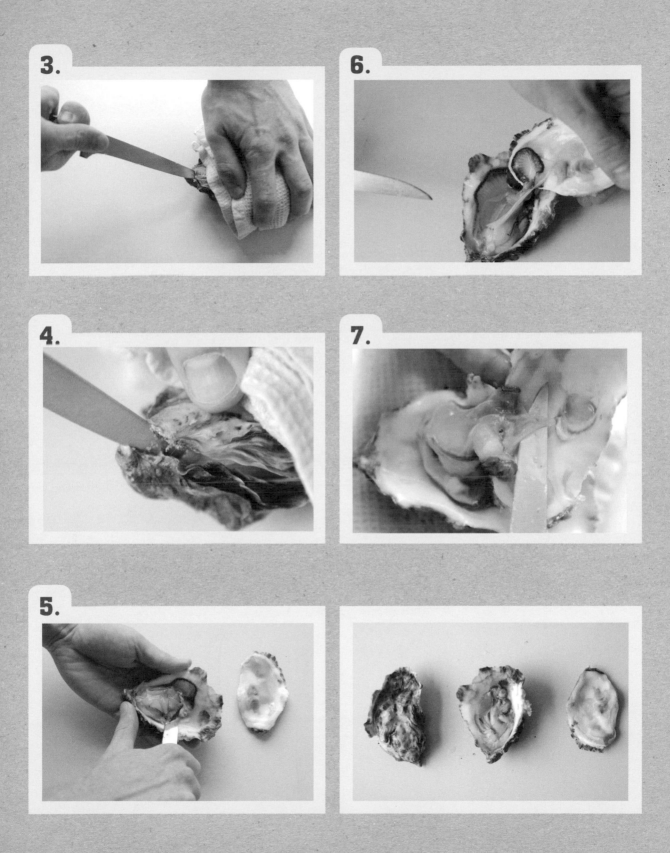

3.

6.

4.

7.

5.

THE PADI SCUBA CERTIFICATE SYSTEM GOES LIKE THIS:

Open Water Diver (max. 18m depth in open water i.e the sea)

Advanced Open Water Diver (max. 30m depth)

Rescue Diver

Dive Master (able to lead qualified divers and assist teaching)

Instructor

SEA SAFETY

AS MUCH AS WE LOVE the water, it can also be a dangerous thing if it isn't treated with respect. So the next few pages will give you some key knowledge which will allow you to enjoy the sea without worry.

TIDES AND WAVES

Whether we use the sea for pleasure, or like some, as a source of income, it's important to understand the different tidal and wave conditions and know how they can affect us, both in terms of our safety and our potential enjoyment.

Tides and waves are some of the most potent and powerful forces on our Earth and are responsible for moving trillions of gallons of water, eroding millions of miles of coastline and have the potential to supply us with an environmentally friendly source of power for the future.

The tides are caused by the gravitational pull of the moon and sun combined. When the moon and sun are lined up with the earth, they create large 'spring' tides – this is when the tide's range is at its maximum and currents are strongest. When the sun and earth are at right angles to each other, the forces aren't in alignment, and smaller 'neap' tides are formed, where the tidal range is at a minimum. Tide times can be predicted accurately: when the tides will be high and low, as well as how high or low, in a particular location at a particular time. Take the tide times for Penzance on 15th June, 2011 for example:

WED 15 JUN

HW	LW	HW	LW
03:50	10:31	16:13	22:57
5.3 M	1.0 M	5.4 M	0.9 M

This shows the two high tides during the day will be at 03.50 and 16.13 and the height of the tide will be 5.3m and 5.4m and the low tides will be 1.0m and 0.9m. During a spring tide, the difference between high and low tide is greater than during a neap tide. As we can see with Penzance, most bodies of water have a semi-diurnal pattern (i.e. there are two high tides and two low tides every 24 hours).

In actual fact, one tidal day is 24 hrs 50 minutes, meaning that a high tide at 12.00 one day will give the next high tide 12 hours and 25 minutes later (00.25) and the next tide at 12.50 and so on. As the tide comes in or goes out, a tidal current is formed and in some instances can be dangerous. The current will be moving at its fastest halfway between high and low tide.

When you're doing an activity by the sea, it's essential to know...

1. What the tide is doing (coming in/ going out).

2. When the next high or low tide is.

3. How high the next tide is and whether this will affect what you are doing.

Once, without properly checking the tides, Thom, Trevor and I put all of our lobster pots one afternoon into a nice rocky spot, planning to leave them overnight. Not realising the tides were big spring tides, we watched that evening as the pots disappeared off to the horizon, never to be seen again. The rope we had used was too short to let the pots rest on the sea's bottom and the marker buoys dragged them off with the rising tide. An expensive mistake.

WAVES

One of the funniest things I've ever seen was watching Trevor, a 6'3" tall Dutchman, dressed in a wetsuit and hood, completely taken out by a wave. The funniest about it was that Trev was standing on dry sand at the time, gutting two mullet we'd just caught. He saw the wave coming and tried to jump it, only to have the enormous beachbreaker land on him, making him do a back flip, and ending up on his arse. He did hang onto the fish, but showed us all the immense power of a big wave.

All we say is this: if you don't feel comfortable in the sea, and the waves are bigger than you can handle, get out of the water. Waves can be dangerous, but there are other factors that can make the situation worse: fear and accompanying panic. As a pretty inexpert surfer, with friends who are far better than me and often lead me out into waves larger than I can surf, I've been in the 'washing machine' far too many times. But I'm OK with it. I relax and tell myself everything will be all right. After I have been tumbled by a wave, I swim for the surface and get ready to take a big breath. Understanding yourself and the conditions you are in is a big part of feeling comfortable in the sea. Confidence takes a long time to build up and can quickly be shattered. If a wave is coming towards you, looking like it will break on top of you, duck dive through the face of the wave. As the fastest moving part of the wave is at the top, diving down through the bottom will see you emerge happily at the other side.

We advise people to take their time with waves and build up to the big stuff gradually – oh yes, and one more thing: never gut your mullet by the shore breakers on Gwenver beach (Trevor).

RIPS & FLAGS

I have seen the wonderful people at the RNLI (Royal National Lifeboat Institution) plus boats and helicopters in action three times and hope I never have to see it again. I tell people about what I saw not to shock, but to try and push home the point that although the ocean is wonderful, awe-inspiring and to be enjoyed, it has also taken many, many lives. So to stay safe by the sea, there are some rules that need to be followed and some things that all ocean users should know. Not following the rules doesn't make us extreme or awesome, it makes us selfish and risks not only our lives, but also those around us and those of our potential rescuers. I know surfers, divers, beach-goers and even walkers who have died in the ocean and all of them were experienced sea-goers.

RIP CURRENTS

A rip current is a strong channel of water, flowing out to sea from near the shore, generally on the surf line. That water can flow at anything between 0.5 – 8 m/s. This is substantially faster than most of us can swim and so getting stuck in a rip current will see us disappearing to the horizon at a rate of knots. On a day where the surf is big, the rip is bigger. Getting caught in a rip current, even on a surfboard, can be a frightening and exhausting experience. Rip currents can be unpredictable and change positions on the beach as the tides change, so safe swimming water one day might be a deadly rip the next. For this reason, we strongly recommend that you only swim at beaches with RNLI Lifeguard support. Lifeguards are some of the best watermen and women, with experience and respect for the oceans and what the oceans can do. There will normally be a board near the entrance to the beach, showing when the beach is lifeguarded i.e. between which hours, plus other useful information on tides. Most of the big, popular beaches will be well guarded.

If you do get stuck in a rip, swimming back towards land will only tire you out. The rip is like a treadmill which you need to get off. So, swim sideways, parallel to the beach, towards the end where you can see the most people.

If you are unable to swim out of it, try and stay calm, taking deep breaths. Exhaustion is the enemy here, so if you can preserve your energy by keeping calm then do so. Wave both hands above your head and shout for help, raising the attention of the lifeguard. Very soon you should have someone coming out to bring you back to safety.

If you can stand, then wade along the beach instead of swimming.

If you can see someone else in trouble, then get a lifeguard or call 999 or 112, asking for the coastguard.

FLAGS

There are only three flags to remember, which makes things very simple. These flags mark out who can use what area on a beach, where's safe to go and where's not.

Red and Yellow Flags – Lifeguarded area. Safest area to swim, body board and use inflatables.

Black and White chequered – For surfboards, stand-up paddleboards, kayaks, and other non-powered craft. Launch and recovery area for kite surfers and windsurfers. Not for swimmers, body boarders or inflatable crocodiles. I have been in a black and white area, after notifying the lifeguard, to photograph surfers. Even with fins, mask, a helmet and full wetsuit on, I got in the way. When you have a camera in the surf, people tend to surf at you. Luckily I could see the men on boards fly past above me and all was well. But I got tired much quicker than normal and it was a long swim home.

Solid Red - Never go in the water under any circumstances when the red flag is flying. These flags mark out rocks, dangerous currents, rough seas or other hazards that are likely to endanger anyone that enters the water.

SOME THINGS THAT MIGHT BITE OR STING YOU IN THE SEA, AND WHAT TO DO IF IT HAPPENS

Some animals don't go for the big, scary, hairy, toothy thing. They find all of that a bit obvious. These cunning organisms opt instead to poison, sting or stun those around them either in self-defense, or in attack. The pain from a sting is caused by venom, which contains a concoction of different chemicals, entering the body. When trying to find a remedy for a bite or a poison, we're looking for a reaction or treatment that can neutralise or deactivate the painful chemicals. Below are a few creatures that might sting, and what to do when on the receiving end.

Weever Fish *(Echiichthys vipera)*

I've spent a great deal of time, barefoot and shin deep in the sea and in my 29 years of ocean frolicking have only been struck by a weever fish once. We British tend to have an irrational fear of fish lurking in the deep out to get us but, in reality, fish will get the hell out of our way rather than get squashed. Normally we're stung as a last resort as happened to me one sunny day in July a couple of years ago, on Sennen beach in Cornwall, when I stood on a weever fish. It stuck its spiky, poisoned dorsal fin into the sole of my foot to protect itself. The poison that leeched into the soft tissue on the under-sole of my foot was initially masked by the numbness from the cold sea. When leaving the water, the stinging sensation began to intensify, building to a nasty bee-sting-like throb. Once I'd noticed it half way up the beach, it had worsened, numbing my foot to give a fairly decent pain.

What to do: plunge your foot in as hot water as is bearable (careful not to burn yourself!) until the water becomes cool. Repeat until the pain has gone. The protein-based venom of the weever sting becomes denatured and stops working on our nerve cells when it gets hot. It's a bit like cooking the white of an egg. Just as the white turns from a clear jelly to white solid by heating it, so it is true of the poison; heat it until the toxin denatures and stops working on you.

Jellyfish *(Cnidaria)*

The problem we may have with jellyfish and their nematocyst stinging cells is that they are generally small, fairly hard to see and, when they are about, they come en masse. The jellyfish sting feels like the injection you get at the dentist, followed by numbness; a kind of unpleasant, sharp, needle-like scratching which dies away, leaving a feeling that part of your skin has been drinking a bit too much.

What to do: everyone knows that if you get stung by a jellyfish, you've got to pee on yourself. Right? Wrong! In fact, contrary to what you've heard, you SHOULD NOT PEE on jellyfish stings as it can make it worse. Weak vinegar, ethanol (vodka) or seawater are the best tonics, but only on some groups of jellyfish. Others, like the Portuguese Man o' War, are actually unrelated to these normal jellyfish. If you are stung by a jellyfish, your best bet is to seek medical attention and try to note the key identifying feature of any jellyfish present, as it will help with treatment. (This goes with all stings, bites and brushes with bushes.)

Urchins *(Echinoidea)*

Starfish (sea stars), brittle stars, sea cucumbers and sand dollars are all relatives of these spiky little balls of fun found in most coastal waters of the world. Some species do make a unique edible delicacy and are top of the Japanese 'eat it raw' list. With a consistency like mushy oranges and a flavour similar to a mild fishy caviar, the sea urchin is not totally unpleasant to eat, but gets its own back by managing to get itself under the feet of plenty of holiday makers each year. Only about ten species offer any kind of chemical toxin worth worrying about, but the spines can pierce skin and cause infection if not removed. Urchin spines are made from a magnesium-rich calcium carbonate, a material used by lots of marine animals (corals, gastropods etc). The spines can be very painful when stuck in your foot and are quite tricky to remove, like a massive splinter.

What to do: if you do get an urchin spine stuck in your flesh, remove as much as possible with a clean pair of tweezers. This can be painful but is essential. Then soak the puncture wound in neat vinegar and wait. The spine will react with the acidic vinegar and should dissolve in front of your eyes! It may take a few goes and may sting, but better that than a foot infection. Then, I would wash your foot with an alcohol-based hand sanitiser, to keep the bacteria out and make it smell nice in the process.

The trip of a life time...

I have travelled the globe in search of underwater adventure, but I don't think I will ever top a three-month, drawn out series of highs that I had along South Africa's east coast. I headed to South Africa in June in the hope of seeing one of the greatest natural marine events in the world, the Sardine Run. This phenomenon happens each year, when sardines gather in immense numbers, with shoals reaching 15km long and 2km wide, and migrate up the coast to warmer waters to breed. Not only is this an incredible sight in itself, but when you combine about a trillion sardines with all the things that love to feed on them, you have something truly spectacular: a theatrical show of dive bombing gannets, nimble, darting sharks, dolphins and gargantuan whales.

My trip started in the cold waters of Gansbaii, a small fishing town two hours east of Cape Town that just so happens to have quite a substantial population of Cape Fur seals on the nearby Dyer Island. And these seals just so happen to be the main food source of what I consider to be the most awesome predator in the ocean – or possibly on the whole planet for that matter – the Great White Shark.

I was lucky enough to see Great Whites of up to 4 metres long (from inside the safety of a metal cage!) though they have been recorded at over 6 metres in length. I can only describe them as being like trains in the water. They are unbelievably thick-set, muscular and powerful, yet graceful all at once. There are only really three places in the world that offer a regular chance of seeing them, South Australia, California, and South Africa, with the latter offering the best chances of seeing them (almost 100%) at the most affordable price (about £100 for a day trip).

Heading further up the coast, my next amazing experience occurred at Aliwal Shoal, a long reef just south of Durban. I originally went there for some tiger shark diving (no cage this time), but ended up getting more than I bargained for. On day one, I went out with the most reputable tiger shark diving company, Blue Wilderness, as a paying punter. But I soon got deep into conversation with the boat's skipper (and owner), swapping diving stories. Before I knew it, he had invited me back to his house, where I met a couple of the world's most famous underwater camera experts: Thomas Peschak, known for his infamous shot of a Great White following a yellow kayak (you can see this at www.thomaspeschak.com) and Didier Noirot, an unbelievable French videographer who travelled with Jacques Cousteau on the 'Calypso', filming his adventures, and then went on to film the BBC's award winning 'Planet Earth' and 'Blue Planet' series. These guys are legends in the marine photography world, and were in the area to try and capture the Sardine Run on film, and here I was having a beer and a barbeque with them. But the fun had only just begun. What happened the next day was an experience beyond words, and though I will try and explain, I can't even come close to expressing what it felt like on the day.

An early start and our RIB had accelerated from 0-50mph in a flash, punching its way through six-foot waves with ease. Once past the breakers, there was only a breath of wind and the flat calm water allowed us to see our first magical sight of the day, a massive spout of water in the distance, signifying the presence of a whale.

We got to our destination on Aliwal Shoal, and anchored a 'bait stem' at a depth of five metres, from a large buoy on the surface. Our bait stem was made from the drum of an old washing machine with a hinged door fitted, its centre filled with sardine bait, the idea being that the sea's current would take the scent across the reef, drawing sharks from the surrounding area. Within minutes, there seemed to be sharks everywhere, including Black Tip Reef sharks up to an amazing 1.6 metres in length – but it was another type of shark that we were waiting for.

Suddenly, the skipper who had had his eyes fixed on the water throughout, turned to us and shouted, 'Tiger, we've got a Tiger!', and the whole boat was bustling with action as everyone prepared their kit. Within a minute we were all in the water and the cameras were rolling, as Didier captured stock footage to use in his 'National Geographic' documentary. These creatures were amazing, beautifully striped with square, blunt noses – totally unmistakable. I soon realised that there was a hierarchy of respect among the sharks, with the Black Tips still buzzing around but giving the cruising Tiger shark some space. On Didier's recommendation, I had got into the water without scuba equipment as he said that if I wanted to get some 'real' interactions, I must ditch the bubbles. I am reasonably fit, and the more I relax the longer I can stay underwater, but the minute or so I managed right up next to the shark was quite long enough for me! Soon, the Tiger drifted off and, happy with the footage he'd got, Didier decided it was time to have some real fun. He set up his huge old 'workhorse' camera before saying, 'Thom, you are the model! Get in the water, and Marc-ous (the skipper, Marcus, In Didier's French accent), you throw sardines at him!' The guy has worked with Jacques-bloody-Cousteau, so what am I going to do? Argue with him?!

So there I was, in the water, when Marcus, using an old diving flipper, began scooping sardines out of a large black bin into the water. Didier started rolling the camera and then got into the water, dropping down a few metres below us to film from underneath. The sardines started raining down on the water a metre or two in front of me, and then the sharks began a feeding frenzy. I got the odd 'bump' as a Black Tip quickly turned to snatch the nearest free offering, hopefully aware that I was not about to fight him for his dinner. Just as I started getting into it and enjoying myself, I saw Didier rising through the clear water, shaking his head and cursing. Was it something I had done? No. He headed straight for the surface to have words with Marcus. 'Mar-cous! I told you to throw the f*$!ing sardines AT Thom, not 2 metres away! Merde!' Then his regulator was back in place and he was in the water once more. I took a deep breath and waited, knowing that things were going to get pretty intense. The sharks waited too, circling for their next snack. And then the sardines rained in all around me and very quickly just as many sharks to match. I remember closing my eyes at one point, just waiting for the inevitable bite. But it never came. Still the sardines rained down. Plop, plop, plop, plop. I was getting bumped quite a lot now, and I swirled around in the vortexes of their powerful tails as they rushed towards each bit of new bait that arrived. When I did open my eyes, I could barely see a thing for the mass of blurred sharks, foam and silver scales as they demolished the last bin load of fish. But once the food was gone, they sloped off into the blue. Didier surfaced once again and seemed quite pleased. I was quiet, still unsure whether that was the best or most stupid thing I'd ever done...

We then pulled the bait stem up and were about to head home for a well-earned beer and a look over the footage when Didier, a strange look on his face as he scanned the water, started muttering something about whales. We had seen them much further out to sea that day and, although I didn't know much about them, I did know that they were notoriously shy and difficult to get close to, so thought our chances were very slim.

Then suddenly, Didier shouted, 'Yes! Just there!' and everyone on the boat lurched forward as the brakes were slammed on, and the Frenchman was pointing to a disturbance on the water only 100m in front of us.

I asked what we were going to do, hoping and praying that the answer was to get in the water and see these monster Humpback whales up close. Didier was no longer in his wetsuit but the photographer and I were still suited up, so Didier gave us tips from his previous experiences: 'You must swim very smoothly – if you splash your fins, they will be gone!'

We gently slipped into the water and headed off in what he hoped was the right direction. Time seemed almost to stop as the two of us swam slowly forward, eyes hardly blinking, hoping to catch a tiny glimpse of the whales before they vanished.

And then it happened. Through the incredibly clear water, a dark shape came into view. As each gentle leg stroke brought me closer, an enormous Humpback whale came into focus and I could not believe what I was seeing. The water was about 15m deep, and a full grown, 12-metre Humpback whale was lying perfectly vertical and motionless in the water, his nose hovering about two metres off the sandy bottom, his tail just under the surface. It almost looked as if he was asleep and it was the most bizarre thing I think I have ever seen. My heart was absolutely racing, so my breath didn't last long, and I was back at the surface needing more air in no time. I had to calm down if I was to get a decent amount of time up close, but I was so nervous that he could wake at any time and be gone. After a minute, I had gathered some composure and I dived under once more, this time spending just under a minute swimming round this amazing animal, so close that I could see all the barnacles growing on him. The photographer got some great shots and then, to make it even more special, another whale turned up, nudged mine as if to wake him up, before the two of them circled round for a few minutes and then headed off into the blue, never to be seen again. It was the most special five minutes of my diving career and topped off a day that I will never forget.

HOW TO GUT A FISH

1.

Wash the fish under a cold tap to remove any debris/excess slime. Dry the fish (and your hands) well and lay the fish on newspaper, on top of a chopping board with the tail closest to you and the head furthest away

2.

Insert the knife into the anal opening (found on the underneath of the fish, towards the tail), about 10-15mm deep. Any deeper and you will begin to cut the guts and this can be a bit smelly.

3.

Holding the fish firmly down on the chopping board with one hand use the knife to cut up the belly towards the 'chin' using a gentle sawing motion, being careful not to insert the knife too far.

4.

Open the cut you have made and reach up and grab the guts as far towards the throat as possible. There's no easy way to do this; you just have to get stuck in! Use a thin tip knife to cut the gut tract above the area you are holding. Once cut through, all the innards will come away in one piece and leave you with a clean, empty body cavity.

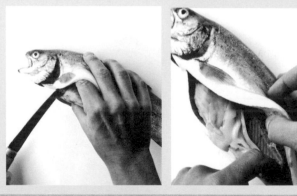

5.

Rinse the fish under the cold tap again and while in the sink, cut down the underside of the backbone now visible in the body cavity. This will be a dark red/purple colour and is the blood found behind the swim bladder. Cut down the length of the backbone and run the back of your thumbnail or a teaspoon down the spine to remove the blood.

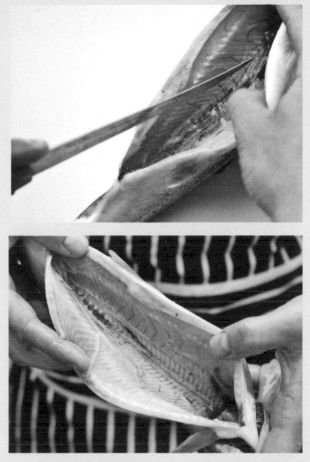

6.

To de-scale, again hold the fish (by the tail) under the cold tap and run a knife at an angle of 90 degrees to the fish in a scraping motion against the grain of the scales, from tail to head. Turn the fish back and forth slightly in the light to see where any scales are you have missed.

7.

The fish is now gutted, de-scaled and prepared for cooking whole, so check out our recipes for cooking fish in foil on pages 36-37, or you can even try doing it in the engine of your car.

HOW TO FILLET A FISH

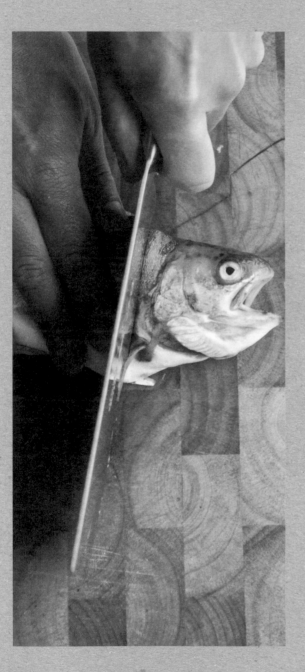

1.

After washing, gutting and de-scaling the fish, dry the fish (and your hands) well or it will slide all over the chopping board! If it is still a bit slippery, fillet the fish on newspaper for more control.

2.

Remove the head by cutting at a slight angle on each side. This makes sure the good flesh behind the head (the 'shoulder') is not lost. Use a heavy knife for this, not your knife for filleting. Your knife for filleting must be as sharp as possible and you do not want to blunt it cutting through the backbone.

3.

Lay the fish flat so it is across you left to right; head at left side if you're left handed, right side if you're right handed, and hold down firmly. Put the knife horizontally on the upper side of the central backbone. Keeping the knife flat to the bone, cut from head to tail end. As you cut you will feel the knife ping through bones that radiate out from the backbone, these will be removed later. Try to keep the motion of the knife smooth, this will avoid hacking the delicate flesh.

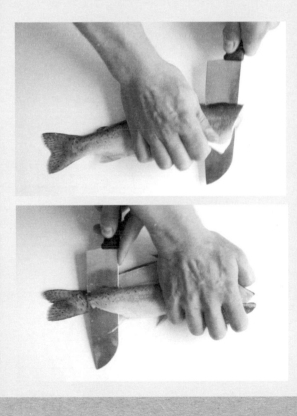

4.

Once you have cut the fillet from the body, turn the fillet over. There are two sets of bones that you have cut through that radiate out from the backbone. One set is the ribcage that is very shallow in the flesh and can be easily sliced out from the fillet. The second set of bones – the pin bones – need to be removed by gently running the back of the knife down the fillet, from head to tail. This will lift the end of the bones slightly and make them more visible to remove with tweezers. Feel gently with the fingertips for remaining bones. You will be left with a perfect, boneless fillet to enjoy.

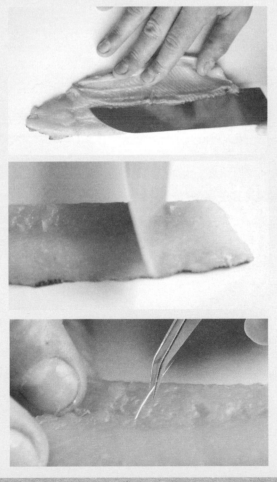

FISH ID

WHAT'S WHAT UNDER WATER

We love spending time under, on, in, near, or thinking about being near Britain's wonderful different bodies of water. Whether Thom is dreaming of chucking some flies for jumping brown trout, Tim is snorkelling in calm Cornish seas or Trev with trousers rolled up to his knees is dipping for edible crabs, you can be sure that we've always got water on our mind. Knowing what you're looking at when you've caught a whopper can take a little skill and we thought we'd whip together a guide of all the likely blighters you may see or encounter when snorkelling, fishing or mucking about near the sea or in fresh water. It's not a comprehensive guide to everything out there, but includes the things you are most likely to encounter if and when you go looking.

NOTE - For some of the animals here, there are more than one species in one family, often called by the same common name (for example there are 20 different species of Goby in the UK but we tend to call them all Goby (*Gobiidae*). Where we can, we've put the Latin name of the most likely you'll come across or just the name of the family. Using Latin names lets us know exactly which species or family of animals we're looking at and is the same across all languages. What we in Britain call a 'snail' is '*un escargot*' in French, but, in both English and French, a common garden snail is *Helix aspersa* – no confusion possible.

You may only ever be so lucky to see some of these in the fishmonger's on ice but it's worth knowing what the thing you're eating looks like. Follow the guide and tick them off as you see them face-to-face in the water or catch them for your tea.

ANGLER/MONK FISH *Lophius piscatorius*

Habitat	Marine – sandy/shell/gravel bottoms
Life Strategy	Carnivorous ambush predators using a dangly lure to entice a wide range of smaller fish over its huge teeth-filled mouth
Best caught	Not targetable by rod and line fishing. Caught off shore by indiscriminately trawling the seabed
Edibility rating	Yum yum
Size Range	1 - 15lbs
Target Size	3lbs
Notes	We've put the angler fish (or monk fish at the fishmongers) in because it shows the great range of fish we have in the UK. As an ambush predator that can live in very deep water off shore, you're unlikely to catch one

BARBEL *Barbus barbus*

Habitat	Rivers, very occasionally stocked lakes
Life Strategy	Bottom feeding – torpedo shape suits fast flowing stretches of river
Best caught	Ledgering luncheon meat over a bed of hemp
Edibility rating	Bit rank
Size Range	5 - 20lbs
Target Size	8lbs
Notes	Use strong tackle! We reckon probably the most hard fighting freshwater fish

BREAM *Abramis brama*

Habitat	Lakes, Rivers, Canals
Life Strategy	Shoaling omnivore
Best caught	Juveniles ('skimmers', less than 1lbs) float fish in mid-water/ bottom with maggots. Mature adults with swim feeder/ground bait/maggots/ worms/sweet corn
Edibility rating	Only when there's nothing else
Size Range	8oz - 18lbs
Target Size	3lbs

BROWN TROUT *Salmo trutta*

Habitat	Rivers, Sea, Lakes
Life Strategy	Carnivore – eating insects and their larvae
Best caught	Fly fishing in spring/ early summer
Edibility rating	Yum yum
Size Range	4oz - 10lbs
Target Size	1.5lbs

CARP *Cyprinus carpio*

Habitat	Lakes – occasionally slow moving rivers/ canals
Life Strategy	Opportunist – greedy little things – will eat pretty much anything
Best caught	Ledgering with luncheon meat, pellets, boilies or sweetcorn
Edibility rating	Edible
Size Range	5 - 50lbs
Target Size	10lbs

CHUB *Leuciscus cephalus*

Habitat	Rivers, occasionally canals/lakes
Life Strategy	Jack of all trades – will eat most things
Best caught	Float fishing/ ledgering with maggots or bread especially in areas of cover where chub like to hide
Edibility rating	Emergency only
Size Range	1 - 9lbs
Target Size	3lbs
Notes	Catchable even in the winter when most other species aren't feeding

COD *Gadus morhua*

Habitat	Deep water fish except in winter where populations migrate to inshore waters and into estuaries
Life Strategy	Opportunistic shoaling bottom feeders
Best caught	Shore fishing with lugworm/ peeler crab on a ledger rig over shingly bottoms at night. Boat fishing in deeper water over rocky bottoms
Edibility rating	Yum yum
Size Range	2 - 35lbs
Target Size	8lbs

COMMON SOLE *Solea solea*

Habitat	Marine/ inshore, sandy and muddy bottoms in shallow water. Occasionally in estuaries
Life Strategy	Nocturnal scavenger/ hunter eating worms and crustaceans
Best caught	At night, ledgering on sandy beaches
Edibility rating	Yum yum
Size Range	up to 4lbs
Target Size	2lbs

CONGER EEL *Conger conger*

Habitat	Marine – wrecks and reefs, loves a good nook and cranny. Moves deeper with age
Life Strategy	Top dog of the rock pool, eating anything else in it. Nocturnal feeders
Best caught	You need the strongest tackle and big hooks! They live in amongst rocky ground and wrecks, and these are powerful creatures. Use a whole mackerel as bait
Edibility rating	Not one that I've ever eaten – a fish to release once caught
Size Range	5 - 100lbs
Target Size	10lbs

EEL *Anguilla anguilla*

Habitat	From the Sargasso Sea in the Atlantic to rivers and lakes. Even travelling over land
Life Strategy	Opportunistic nocturnal scavengers
Best caught	At night - ledgering worms or dead fish heads
Edibility rating	Not bad – one of the better freshwater fish to eat
Size Range	12oz – 8lb
Target Size	2lb

Angler/Monk Fish
SALTWATER

Chub
FRESHWATER

Goby
SALTWATER

Cod
SALTWATER

Grey mullet
SALTWATER

Barbel
FRESHWATER

Common Sole
SALTWATER

Bream
FRESHWATER

Gurnard
SALTWATER

Brown Trout
FRESHWATER & SALTWATER

Conger Eel
SALTWATER

Haddock
SALTWATER

Carp
FRESHWATER

Eel
FRESHWATER & SALTWATER

(Lesser spotted)
Dogfish
SALTWATER

Garfish
SALTWATER

Mackerel
SALTWATER

Rainbow Trout
FRESHWATER

Sea bass
SALTWATER

Perch
FRESHWATER

Roach
FRESHWATER

Sea Scorpion
SALTWATER

Pike
FRESHWATER

Rockling
SALTWATER

Tench
FRESHWATER

Plaice
SALTWATER

Rudd
FRESHWATER

Turbot
SALTWATER

Pollock
SALTWATER

Scad
SALTWATER

Wrasse
SALTWATER

GARFISH *Belone belone*

Habitat	Marine – surface-living offshore species, which come inshore during summer and autumn
Life Strategy	Predator of silver fish such as sand eels
Best caught	By our good friend Pumpy, who can only catch garfish. Float fishing with mackerel strips shallow (up to 4ft deep)
Edibility rating	Pretty delicious
Size Range	Species dependent. Can range from about 1/2lb up to 2lbs
Target Size	1lb
Notes	When cooked, garfish have green bones. Don't be put off, they are pretty tasty

GOBIES *Gobiidae (family)*

Habitat	Marine and estuarine: living in rock pools in intertidal zones
Life Strategy	Hiders. These are the ultimate prey and are eaten by pretty much everything. As a result have very good camouflage
Best caught	With a net and a bucket!
Edibility rating	Pretty delicious
Size Range	Species dependent. Most less than 5oz. Up to 1/2lbs
Target Size	1 inch plus – they're all tiny!
Notes	There are nearly 200 species of gobies and they all look very similar. You'd have to be a goby expert to tell them apart. Our favourite is the Two Spotted Goby

GREY MULLET *Mugilidae (family)*

Habitat	Marine – inshore, living close into the shoreline and around features such as harbours or footings
Life Strategy	Benthic filter feeders, filtering through nutrient rich mud on sea beds for worms and small crustaceans
Best caught	Float fishing with bread in harbours
Edibility rating	Yum yum
Size Range	1 – 10lbs
Target Size	3lbs
Notes	Mullet will taste of what they live in. Catch them in a harbour and they'll be pretty rank. Catch them in the open ocean and they'll be delicious. They are probably one of our favourite eating fish

GURNARDS *Triglidae (family)*

Habitat	Marine: found in inshore waters. Found over all types of seabed
Life Strategy	Eats mainly bottom-feeding invertebrates such as shrimp and small crabs. The red gurnard is the most active of the family
Best caught	Not fussy: caught on or near bottom of sea with pretty much any bait. Worm or squid is a favourite
Edibility rating	Yum yum
Size Range	Dependent on species. Up to 3lbs
Target Size	1lb

HADDOCK *Melanogrammus aeglefinus*

Habitat	Marine – lives close to sea beds between depths of 40 and 300m
Life Strategy	Bottom feeder, eats mainly invertebrates and few fish
Best caught	Out on a boat
Edibility rating	Awesome – one of the best
Size Range	1–10lbs
Target Size	4lbs

(Lesser spotted) DOGFISH *Scyliorhinus canicula*

Habitat	Marine – bottom dwelling, over sand/ fine gravel. Inshore up to 100m deep. Often found on sandy spots between rocky outcrops when snorkelling
Life Strategy	Bottom feeding predators, feeding on invertebrates in sand
Best caught	When ledgering with worms/squid/ mackerel as bait – more often than not when you are fishing for something else. Dogfish will pester you!
Edibility rating	Better than average
Size Range	1–3lbs
Target Size	1.5lbs
Notes	Can be caught by hand (which we've done). Called rock salmon when served, although skin is incredibly tough to get off. You also need to put them in the freezer for a couple of weeks to get rid of the ammonia in their bodies

MACKEREL *Scomber scombrus*

Habitat	Marine: Winter, deep waters; Summer, inshore waters
Life Strategy	Shoaling pelagic fish, feeding on small fry/mid-water plankton/small crustaceans
Best caught	Boat fishing with white feathers. From piers using feathers/spinners. (See Thom's top mackerel fishing tips)
Edibility rating	Yum yum
Size Range	8oz - 1.5lbs
Target Size	1lbs
Notes	Juveniles are called 'joey' mackerel

PERCH *Perca fluviatilis*

Habitat	Lakes, Rivers, Canals
Life Strategy	Aggressive carnivore and predator – lives anywhere there are shoaling fry
Best caught	Float fishing/ledgering with a big, juicy lob worm under overhanging trees or near reed beds
Edibility rating	Emergency only
Size Range	4oz - 5lbs
Target Size	2lbs
Notes	When holding perch always push the dorsal fin backwards as it is very sharp

PIKE *Esox lucius*

Habitat	Lakes, Rivers, Canals
Life Strategy	Aggressive; top carnivore and ambush predator – lives anywhere where there are smaller fish
Best caught	Livebaiting with small (around 4" long) fish
Edibility rating	Edible
Size Range	2 - 45lbs
Target Size	10lbs (max 65cm for eating)

PLAICE *Pleuronectes platessa*

Habitat	Marine – sandy bottoms, both in and offshore waters. Moving into the intertidal zone with a rising tide
Life Strategy	Feeds on crustaceans and molluscs buried in the sand. Adapted to snip the siphons of buried molluscs
Best caught	Spear fishing /float fishing with mackerel strips or lure fishing off the rocks
Edibility rating	Yum yum
Size Range	1 - 2lbs
Target Size	1.5lbs

POLLOCK *Pollochius pollochius*

Habitat	Marine: inshore near rocks and over rough ground when younger, move deeper with age
Life Strategy	Ambush predators – attack small shoals of fry from below. (You can see this when snorkelling)
Best caught	Spear fishing /float fishing with mackerel strips or lure fishing off the rocks
Edibility rating	Better than average
Size Range	2-20lbs
Target Size	3lbs with spear/ 8lbs with rod

RAINBOW TROUT *Oncorhynchus mykiss*

Habitat	Lakes – occasionally slow moving rivers/canals
Life Strategy	Opportunist – greedy little things – will eat pretty much anything
Best caught	Ledgering with luncheon meat, pellets, boilies or sweetcorn
Edibility rating	Edible
Size Range	5 - 50lbs
Target Size	10lbs

ROACH *Rutilus rutilus*

Habitat	Lakes, Rivers, Canals
Life Strategy	Shoaling omnivore – eating passing debris
Best caught	Float fish mid-water/ bottom with maggots/casters/hemp/bread
Edibility rating	Emergency only
Size Range	1oz - 4lbs
Target Size	1lb
Notes	AKA 'Red fins' or 'water sheep'

ROCKLINGS *Gadidae (family)*

Habitat	Marine – rock pools and inshore down to 20m
Life Strategy	Feeding on bottom-loving fish and crustaceans
Best caught	With a net and bucket
Edibility rating	Not worth the bother
Size Range	Species dependent. Most between 1oz - 8oz
Target Size	Generally only a few inches long!

RUDD *Scardinius erythrophthalmus*

Habitat	Lakes, Canals
Life Strategy	Shoaling omnivore – eating passing debris, usually from surface
Best caught	Float fish shallow/ just below surface with maggots/casters
Edibility rating	Emergency only
Size Range	1oz - 4lbs
Target Size	1lb

SCAD *Trachurus trachurus*

Habitat	Marine: offshore rarely deeper than 100m
Life Strategy	Shoaling predators, eating young fish and cephalopods
Best caught	With feathers, as you would mackerel
Edibility rating	Better than average
Size Range	Up to 3 lbs
Target Size	1lb
Notes	AKA as scad mackerel or horse mackerel

SEA BASS *Dicentrarchus labrax*

Habitat	Marine – rocky headlands (fast currents) and large sandy beaches
Life Strategy	Predatory (less than 2lbs are shoaling) carnivores
Best caught	Float fishing/ledgering with live sand eels or lures, fishing off rocky outcrops or ledgering with large squid baits close in – especially in large waves in stormy conditions. Definitely with big bait!
Edibility rating	Yum yum
Size Range	1 - 15lbs
Target Size	3lbs
Notes	Juveniles tend to shoal and are referred to as 'schoolies' (Minimum landing size = 40cm)

SEA SCORPION *Taurulus bubalis*

Habitat	Marine – inshore, living in rocky reefs/ rock pools covered with weed
Life Strategy	Top dog of the rock pool, eating anything else in it
Best caught	N/A – unless by accident!
Edibility rating	N/A
Size Range	max 8 oz
Target Size	N/A

TENCH *Tinca tinca*

Habitat	Lakes, very occasionally slow moving rivers/canals
Life Strategy	Bottom feeders – root around for worms and invertebrates in mud and weed
Best caught	Float fishing at dawn with worms or sweetcorn
Edibility rating	Emergency only
Size Range	2 - 14lbs
Target Size	4lbs

TURBOT *Psetta maxima*

Habitat	Marine – deep water, normally where there is a sandy/shingle bottom. Most common around southerly coast of UK
Life Strategy	Active predator, hunting small fry and shoaling juvenile fish
Best caught	With big fresh bait, from a boat
Edibility rating	Yum yum
Size Range	4-20lbs
Target Size	8lbs
Notes	These guys get really big, we've seen pictures of Turbot that are as big as a small car

WRASSE *Labridae (family)*

Habitat	Marine / Rocky weedy kelpy shorelines
Life Strategy	Crustacean crunchers – have teeth for munching shelled animals off the rocks
Best caught	Ledgering peeler crabs in rocky ground from the shore (N.B. This does lose lots of tackle!)
Edibility rating	Pretty edible
Size Range	8oz - 10lbs
Target Size	3lbs
Notes	Best eaten raw as sashimi with some soya sauce, rice and wasabi

KNOTS

THE KNOTS THAT FOLLOW will come in handy in countless different situations, and if you can master these, you should be pretty much covered.

FISHING KNOTS

Over Hand Loop

A very simple knot to create a loop in the end of a line.

1

Take the end of a piece of line, A, and fold it back on itself to create two parallel lines, B, about 4 inches long.

2

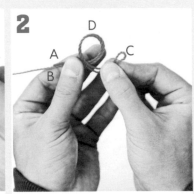

Pinch about 1 inch back from the end of the loop, C, in the right hand with palm facing up, and the end of the line and the line parallel, A & B, in the left hand. Turn the right hand over so palm faces down and bring the two pinched areas together in the left hand. This will create a circular loop, D.

3

Now pass the end of the first loop, C, round the back and through to the front of the circular loop.

4

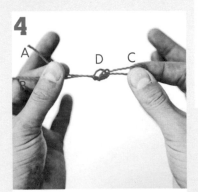

Pull C with your right hand and A and B with your left hand.

5

Pull away from each other and the knot will tighten. DONE!

Turn Blood Knot

This is a strong knot that is easy to tie. It benefits from moistening the knot (saliva will do!) before pulling tight. This reduces the friction on the line that can damage and weaken it.

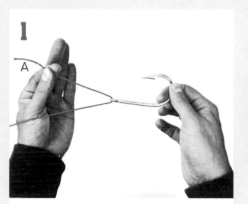

Insert the end of the line, A, through the eye of the hook.

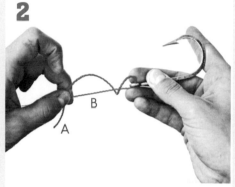

Wrap the end of the line, A, back around the main line, B. Do this 6 times.

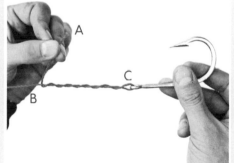

Insert the end of the line, A, through the small loop created when the first wrap is made, C – do not put the line back through the eye of the hook. Pull on the main line to tighten the knot.

Three-Turn Water Knot

For attaching two pieces of line together. Leaves a neat tag piece of line to attach either a mackerel feather or a trout fly.

1

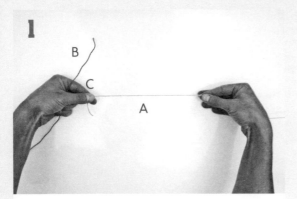

Measure 8 inches back from the end of grey line, A, and pinch between finger and thumb, C. Cut a second piece of line, B (orange line), about 2ft long for feathers, 4ft long for flies.

2

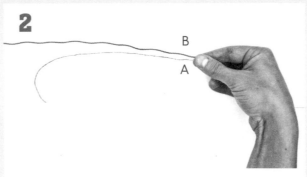

Take one end of line, B, and pinch in the same finger and thumb as A. Lay the lines parallel.

3

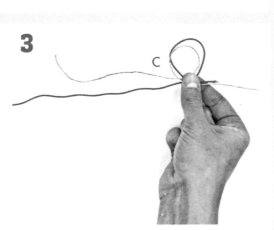

With your left hand, pinch the parallel lines at a point around 4 inches away from the right hand, and roll your left hand over back to C. This will create a loop called an over hand loop. Pinch this loop in your right hand.

4

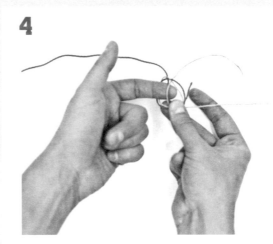

Move the lines ends behind the loop and pass them through the loop. This is best done by hooking the lines on the finger and pulling the line through the loop from the back towards you.

5

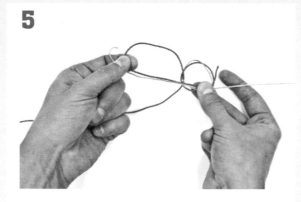

Repeat the move of passing the ends through the loop twice more.

6

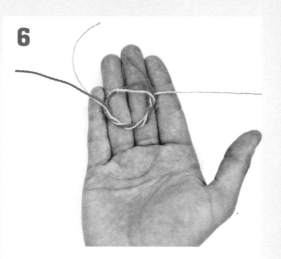

You will now have your three- turn water knot ready to pull tight.

7

Pinch the tag ends and pull away from each other until the knot tightens.

8

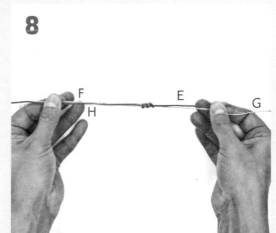

You now have 4 tags coming from the knot. Trim the short orange tag close to the knot, E. Tie a feather or a fly to the grey tag on the left of knot, F (should be 6 inches long). The long grey line goes to the rod, G. Repeat the same knot at the end of the long orange tag for another feather or fly, H.

ROPE KNOTS

Bowline

The best way of making a loop that can be easily undone, even under load.

1

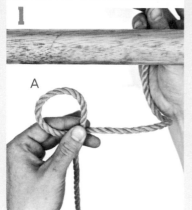

Form a small loop, A, leaving enough remaining rope to go round your pole/tree.

2

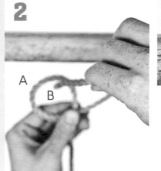

Pass the end of the rope, B, round the pole, and then back through the loop, A.

3

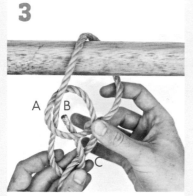

Continue around the main line, C.

4

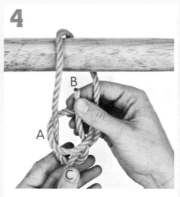

Feed B back through loop A in the opposite direction you have made.

5

Pull the main line, C, tight.

Clove hitch

For hanging buoys, fenders or mackerel from a line or bar; only holds whilst under tension.

1

Pass the end of the rope, A, around the pole.

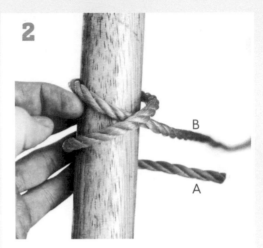

2

Take A over B and around the pole a second time.

3

Thread A under itself.

4

Pull tight.

Reef knot

For connecting the ends of two separate ropes. Gets tighter with added load.

1

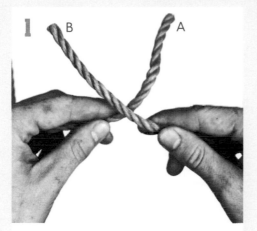

Take the end of each rope and cross the one in your left hand, A, under the one in your right hand, B.

2

Wrap A around B.

3

Cross the rope ends again, A behind B, making a loop.

4

Thread B through the loop.

5

Pull the ends tight.

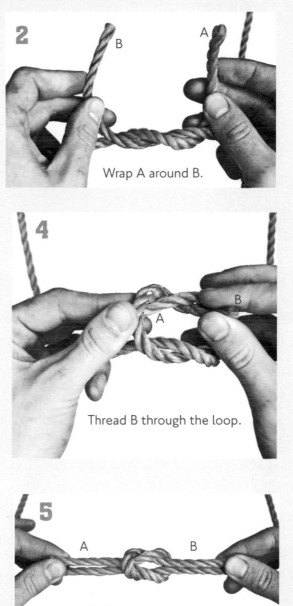

BASIC FISHING RIGS

THE GOOD NEWS IS that there are only three types of rig that you need to master. So, depending on what species you are after, and therefore whether you need to present your bait in mid-water or at the bottom (see our Fish ID section for species' lifestyle/preferred baits), you then just need to follow these tips for a simple, tangle free rig. The only thing to bear in mind is that the size of float, strength of trace and hook should vary depending on the target species and bait used. A good guide is as follows:

❋ The smaller the target species, the more gently they bite, so small fish require smaller, thinner, more delicate floats compared to larger target fish.

❋ Hook sizes are a little bit back to front. For freshwater fishing, the tiniest size (about 5mm long) is a 26 but the largest size is a 2. For sea fishing they start at a 0, and increase in size, going up in increments of one (1/0, 2/0, 3/0) etc right up to humungous hooks for sharks! For small roach, rudd and perch use maggots on size 16-20 hooks; for tench, bream and chub use sweetcorn, luncheon meat and worms on size 10-14 hooks. For large carp, use 4-8 with boilies (boiled paste baits) or multiple corn/worms.

❋ Again, small fish require light lines so start at a 2-3lb line working up to 10-12lb for carp.

BASIC FLOAT RIG

The mainline comes from the rod, and the first part of the rig is the stopper knot (a thin runner band tied onto the line) or gripper bead (available from tackle shops). This sets the depth at which your bait will hang. Usually hanging the bait from half depth down to the bottom is a good place to start.

The float is next and must be buoyant enough to support the bait and be correct for the conditions. For sea fishing (rougher, deep water) and pike fishing (suspending a fish bait) you can get away with a large cigar-shaped float. Then thread some ball weights which will provide casting weight and cock the float at the surface. Next, tie a swivel on using a blood knot

(see Knots section) and, below this, attach the hook length or 'trace'. A trace of between 1-2 ft is a good start. Try to use a trace that is of less strength than the main line. Should you get snagged in weeds or rocks, the trace will break first, meaning that you lose only a hook and not the whole rig. (For pike fishing, you need to use a wire trace or the pike's teeth will bite through it, and a 'treble' hook as pike have very bony mouths so a treble helps keep them on the line. These are pictured parallel to the 'hook length' or 'trace' in the diagram opposite.)

A bite is indicated by a fish bobbing or pulling under the float.

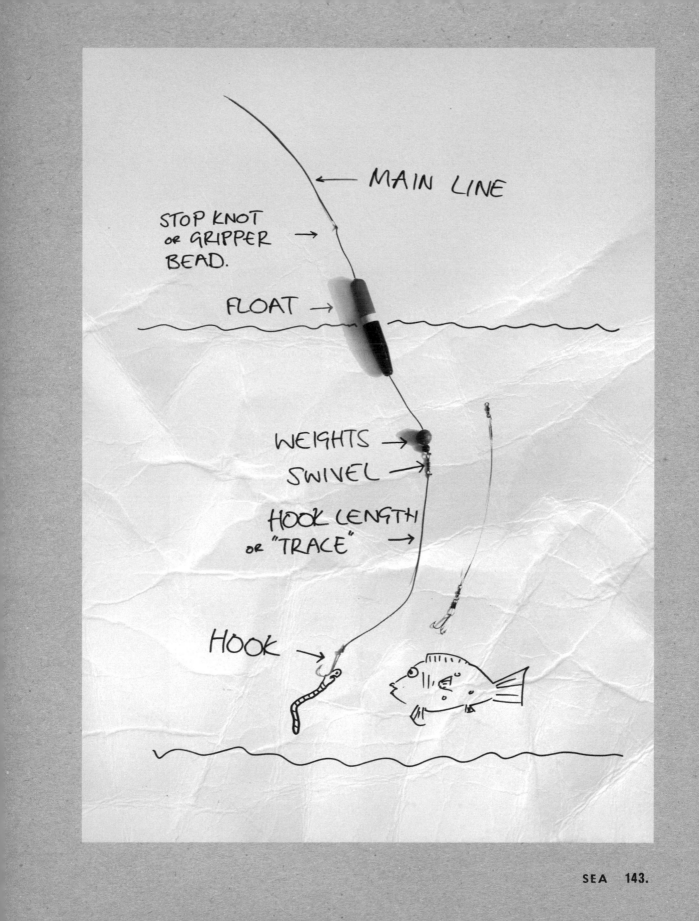

MAIN LINE

STOP KNOT
OR GRIPPER
BEAD.

FLOAT →

WEIGHTS →

SWIVEL →

HOOK LENGTH
OR "TRACE" →

HOOK →

BASIC LEDGER RIG

This rig is designed to present a bait on the bottom of the sea or lake. The main line comes from the rod and threads through a snap swivel, so it is free to run up and down the line without resistance. This snap swivel allows different size weights or 'swim feeders' to be swapped with ease. After the snap swivel a normal swivel should be tied on, which prevents any twist occurring in the line and leads to tangles, and prevents the snap swivel (and weight/swim feeder) sliding down to the hook. At the bottom end of the swivel, the hook length or trace should be added and, finally, a hook to complete the rig. This rig is incredibly simple and tangle free and is great for carp, tench, bream and chub in freshwater, and bass, cod, pollock and conger eels in the sea.

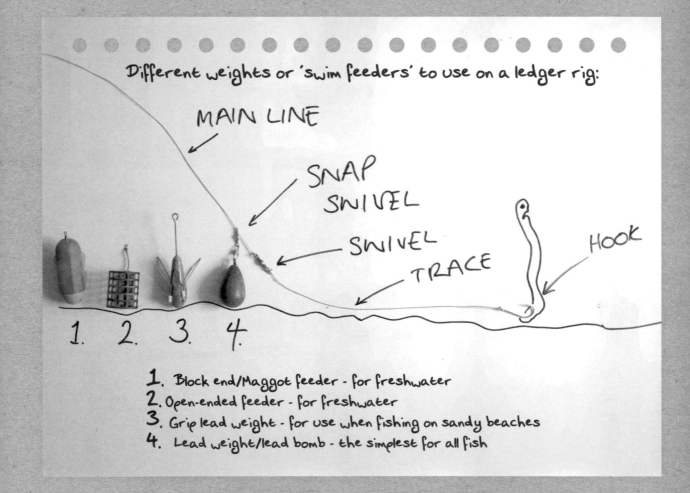

Different weights or 'swim feeders' to use on a ledger rig:

MAIN LINE

SNAP SWIVEL

SWIVEL

TRACE

HOOK

1. 2. 3. 4.

1. Block end/Maggot feeder - for freshwater
2. Open-ended feeder - for freshwater
3. Grip lead weight - for use when fishing on sandy beaches
4. Lead weight/lead bomb - the simplest for all fish

LURE FISHING RIG

The rig is super simple, requiring just one knot to attach the end of your line to a wire trace. A lure is an artificial representation of a bait-fish, so you will use it when you are after predators with teeth! A wire trace with a snap swivel attached (bought ready-made from tackle shops) will stop you getting 'bitten off' and allow you to change the size, shape or colour of lure easily.

These are my top four lures – best used to catch predatory fish: anything from pike and perch in freshwater, to pollack and bass in the sea. For all but the spinner, don't just cast out and wind in. Change the speed of retrieve and flick the rod tip when bringing it in to make the lure more realistic and lifelike.

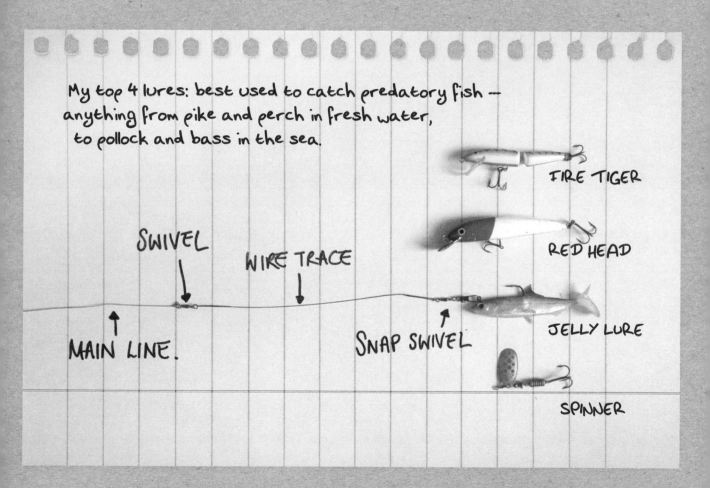

My top 4 lures: best used to catch predatory fish — anything from pike and perch in fresh water, to pollack and bass in the sea.

SWIVEL

WIRE TRACE

MAIN LINE.

SNAP SWIVEL

FIRE TIGER

RED HEAD

JELLY LURE

SPINNER

4. WOODS & FIELDS

WWOOFING: WORKING FOR FREE, BUT FEEDING YOUR BELLY!

ONE VERY POSITIVE WAY that we managed to survive for a small part of our trip in Scotland, was by what is known as WWOOFing. Despite its strange name, this activity does not involve howling like a wolf, acting like a dog or displaying any other canine behaviour, but instead refers to a worldwide movement of volunteers who wish to swap their time, energy and enthusiasm in exchange for accommodation, the gaining of new skills and knowledge. WWOOFing in its early days in the 1970s stood for Willing Workers On Organic Farms but more recently, as the idea had spread around the world, more commonly stands for World Wide Opportunities On Organic Farms.

The concept of working for free might sound a bit odd in these money-mad times but part of what we discovered during the making of our first series was that if both parties involved in the deal are getting something they want out of it, then it's a good one! During filming, we spent a few days at one of the most

beautiful places on the west coast of Scotland called Ardalanish Farm. The farm manager, Roger, allowed us to set up Winnie (our VW van, for those of you who aren't familiar with her) and some tents on a grassy bank overlooking the sea and waking up there was certainly one of the best morning views I've ever seen. The farm has several organic ventures, keeping Kyloe cattle and Hebridian sheep, and keeps several WWOOFers and permanent farm workers busy for large parts of the year. One team of skilled workers is dedicated to weaving wool from the sheep into tweed, preserving the tradition of cloth making for future generations.

During our time in Ardalanish, we were allocated different jobs. I was commissioned to make bobbins, and Thom was initially put onto making labels for the clothes. This proved to be a bit much for his poor eyesight and heavy hand and, after ruining a few, he was given a job he could do with the big man, Trevor: lifting bails of hay. The boys gloated about this one, as they got to spend one of the sunniest days in our whole trip outside, but I feel that I came away having learnt a new skill and with a new appreciation for the craftsmanship that goes into making tweed.

So what did we receive in exchange for our efforts? A little of their prime beef and a spot to camp. Our mouths were watering at the prospect as Roger totted up our share. Unfortunately, just as he was about to hand over £100 worth of beef, the programme's director stepped in. There wouldn't be much 'Hungry' left in the Three Hungry Boys with all that beef! He renegotiated our ration down to three burgers, three steaks and some mince; you can imagine how we cursed.

As we chomped through our burgers that evening, cooked over an open fire as the sun set, the appeal of WWOOFing around the world – picking up skills and the intricate knowledge of organic farming – was definitely not lost on us.

HOW TO WWOOF

Generally, each country has its own WWOOFing organisation which, for a small fee, exists to put 'willing workers' in touch with reliable hosts who will look after and nurture the skills of the volunteer. WWOOFing, like farming, is seasonal and farmers in different parts of the world will require people at different times, depending on their harvest. You can WWOOF in England too. Our friends, Kim and John Coulson at Polgoon Vineyard (**www.polgoonvineyard.vpweb.co.uk**) employ many volunteers seasonally to pick their grapes. I can't imagine that their workers are terribly productive the morning after a night of bubbly but I'm sure that's just one of the perks of the job!

If you want to work in other countries for organic farms, there is a wealth of information online. If you are reliable, willing, cooperative and hardworking then it could be a doorway to a great nomadic few years of adventure.

Go to **www.WWOOF.org** for more details. That's a lot of w's.

FORAGING

FORAGING IS ESSENTIALLY the act of searching for food and provisions in the habitat around you. But before we take you through some delicious and useful plants to forage for, the law.

FORAGING AND THE LAW

I will keep this as concise as possible. No one likes to be force-fed the 'rules'. But important they are, so please humour me for a minute or two. Understanding the laws means you won't have to look over your shoulder or feel uneasy when foraging, and you will know what law to recite if challenged by someone.

First things first. If you do not own the land you are on, you need permission or you will be trespassing. For land owned by the local authorities, wildlife trust, forestry commission etc, there is an implicit permission given for you to be there without any bother. If you do happen to commit the act of trespassing, it is a civil matter not a legal one so you may be asked to leave (which you must do) but you can't be prosecuted for it.

Now moving on to the reason for which you will be on said land: foraging and collecting food. There is a common law that gives people the right to collect the four 'F's – Fruit, Fungi, Flowers and Foliage. Note that this does not include whole plants, so uprooting anything is an offence.

Assuming that you have collected one of the four 'F's, the 1968 Theft Act states that doing this is possible on 'any land' as long as it is 'growing wild' and is not for 'reward, sale or other commercial purpose'. Picking blackberries is fine, as long as they have not been planted specifically (i.e. so long as they are growing wild) or the jam you make is not sold (for reward).

The only time when the above situations are not valid is if a site is covered by CROW (Countryside Rights of Way Act) or if there is a specific by-law in place that prevents the removal of certain (usually rare or endangered) species. This is commonly found on SSSI (Sites of Special Scientific Interest) and there should be notices at the entrance to these areas indicating specific rules.

Lesson over, kids. So back to your happy foraging – hopefully in peace, if you stick to the rules above.

MUSHROOM FORAGING

The last few years has seen us Hungry Boys taking a keen interest in mushroom foraging. And the more we've got into it, the more we've realised that it's a truly huge topic. This is confirmed by the fact that there are lots of very thick books just on the species of mushrooms found in the UK.

Roughly speaking, there are around 4,000 species of the larger fungi in the UK, and should you decide that your life lacks any significant hobbies, you're bored with Jeremy Kyle and his ranting, or you just plain fancy a challenge that ranks next to climbing Everest, you could do worse than attempting to find and catalogue all 4,000. But in true 3HB style, we have provided you with the essentials to have an excellent mushroom foraging experience; and not only have we chosen the most delicious fungi to forage, we have taken into consideration the ease of identification, and relative safety (the chance of mistaking it for something dangerous).

Now, I hate to be the bearer of bad news but it seems that Mother Nature has a funny sense of humour, and for every edible species of mushroom, there is quite often a nasty look-a-like. So the species I have chosen for you here are pretty fail-safe, with just a few simple identifying points to stick to, which will leave you free from problems.

I find the uncertainty often involved in foraging for mushrooms is what makes it so intriguing and rewarding. I would almost put it up there with fishing and shooting as my favourite outdoor activity. It is, in its own way, a form of hunting. It's You vs Nature. You need to know the right places, the right times of year and the right conditions to have success, and just as with other types of hunting, success isn't always guaranteed. Be warned, wild mushroom hunting can get very addictive.

In other countries around Europe, it is possible to take your foraged wild fungi into any pharmacy and they will identify the edible ones for you. Unfortunately, the pharmacies in this country can only provide a long queue behind Doris who needs her angina tablets. But that's what the Three Hungry Boys are here for...

HOW TO IDENTIFY YOUR MUSHROOMS

The outward appearance of a mushroom is not the only thing we can rely on in order to uncover its true identity. There are many other things you must consider too. The type of habitat or substrate on which it is growing – for example oyster mushrooms and velvet shanks grow on dead wood, while St George's grow in fields/pasture land. Any colour changes when damaged or cut: the *Agaricus* genus bruise either red or yellow, and a *Scarletina Bolete* oxidises an intense blue colour when cut. The smell can also give important clues to help identification, as can the colour of the spores the mushroom deposits.

So on the following pages here's our foolproof guide to bagging yourself a self-foraged, delicious and safe mushroom meal.

SO SAFETY FIRST

1.

A little bit of knowledge is a dangerous thing: thinking you know a bit about mushrooms and then getting carried away. There are three routes to safety for the novice mushroom forager, two of which I would recommend. The first option is not to eat any wild mushrooms at all – but I'm not going to suggest that! The second, if your knowledge is limited, is to take great care in fully identifying any possible finds that you might want to eat, and always to err on the side of caution. It is a good idea to have a few foraging trips where the sole purpose is just to see what you find and fully identify the mushrooms, without any consideration for the table just yet. And lastly, if you are short on knowledge (and as a result,

confidence), get some more! With wild food becoming more and more popular, there are lots of really great foraging courses out there that are both fun and informative, and doing one of these is money well spent. The internet can be a huge help too. A quick search can always reveal plenty of forums and photos to help in the identifying process. Check out **www.mushrooms.org.uk** or **www.rogersmushrooms.com** for great photos and identification aids. Also get some field guides for cross-reference. You can definitely do worse than the *Mushrooms: River Cottage Handbook No1* by my good friend John Wright (Bloomsbury, 2007). It helped me massively, and it will help you too.

2.

Don't break the rules! One of the worst rookie mistakes I find people make in identifying mushrooms is making a key feature 'fit' when it really doesn't. An example:

Beginner: 'We found a lovely crop of Chanterelle mushrooms the other day in a field just down the road.'
Me: 'Really? You know chanterelles only grow in woodland. I would double check if I were you'.
Beginner: 'Well, they looked just like them.'

Thinking or believing that your identification is correct, by following some features but ignoring others is a sure-fire way for getting it wrong.

3.

Never pick or eat any mushroom in its juvenile stage. A very young death cap can look remarkably like a small button mushroom that you buy in the supermarket. So steer clear of any mushroom smaller than a ping-pong ball as a rule of thumb.

4.

Lastly, if you're going to keep some specimens for identification later on at home, keep all the definitely edible ones in one basket and separate any 'unknowns' into another basket. Spores from highly poisonous fungi can transfer and contaminate so be safe.

Chanterelle *(Cantharellus cibarius)*

This is my number one mushroom find and probably the most well-known 'wild fungi', after the field mushroom. It has so many great features that finding a glade filled with ripe specimens really is like finding little nuggets of gold. The flesh is firm and delicious, the colour is vibrant and survives the cooking process very well, they are never pestered by bugs and, most importantly, they are easy to identify (with no seriously dangerous imposters). Any stroll around a French supermarket will see punnets of chanterelles for sale (the French are far more adventurous when it comes to eating wild mushrooms). Another great characteristic of the chanterelle is its reliability – it will pop up in the same spot year after year. We Three Hungry Boys are huge supporters of sharing knowledge, but really, if you think I'm pointing you in the direction of my known 'gold digging' spots you are very much mistaken. And I suggest you do the same. If anyone ever asks, just swear blind you've never even eaten, seen or heard of anything known as a chanterelle in your whole life. They really are worth it.

Cap	Yellow, 4-12cm, mostly irregular or wavy edge, flat when young, fluted with a central depression when older
Stem	Varies a lot, yellow with paler areas, usually tapering towards the base
Gills	**Main distinguishing feature:** more like wrinkles and folds than gills, they divide into two
Flesh	Paler than the cap but still yellow
Spore colour	Pale cream to yellow
Smell	Faint fruity smell. Said to smell of apricots when kept in an airtight box
Habitat	Woodland, predominantly beech and oak. Often found on mossy banks
Time of Year	July–first frosts, usually around October

St George's mushroom *(Calocybe gambosum)*

So named because it consistently graces us with its presence on 23rd April, St George's Day. It is white all over: white stem, white cap, white gills (although I really think it could have gone the whole hog and dressed up in a red cross for the occasion). One of the key identifying features of this mushroom is the strong smell of meal/flour it gives off, making it one of those mushrooms where more than just its appearance can help reveal its identity.

The time of year it appears is also quite early in terms of mushroom availability, so it is virtually impossible to mistake it for anything else. Rarely found past the end of May, this is a great mushroom to fill in the spring months, so keep your eyes peeled on walks at this time of year. Found in permanent pasture with relatively short grass; the same fields that you will often find Field, Horse or Macro mushrooms later on in the year.

Cap	White to off white, 6-15cm, domed with slightly rolled edge. Rounder when young, irregular and wavy when mature
Stem	Up to 7cm long and 3cm wide, stocky, white
Gills	White to off white
Flesh	White
Spore colour	White to off white
Smell	**Main distinguishing feature:** smells strongly of fresh meal/flour
Habitat	Grasslands, fields, pasture land, often the same fields you will find horse and field mushrooms later in the year
Time of Year	**Secondary distinguishing feature:** April to May

Cep *(Boletus edulis)*

You can always tell the popularity of something by the number of pet names people have for it. And the Cep is no exception. Also affectionately known as the Penny Bun (the cap looks just like a fresh baked bread roll), the King Bolete, and the exotically well-known name, the Porcini. And its Latin name, *Boletus edulis,* tells us that it is the best member of its *bolete* family to eat. The list of great characteristics that the Cep possesses is long and distinguished, but my favourite is its delicate nutty flavour, with an undisputed depth making it an absolute pleasure when cooked to perfection. But as we know, with every silver lining comes a cloud, and this chap does seem to attract maggots. We humans aren't the only creatures clued up on the Cep's culinary excellence. It therefore helps to pick specimens of a young to medium age. Unless you aren't squeamish, in which case you may want to pick the older mushrooms that have an even more well-developed flavour, but are very likely to contain maggots too.

Cap	Medium to dark brown, looks like a bread roll, hence can reach a magnificent 25cm, mostly up to 15cm though. Domed, hence the name!
Stem	Up to 18cm long and 10cm wide. Quite large compared to the cap, usually swelling towards the base
Gills	Tubes or pores instead of gills. White when young, through to yellow then green when past their culinary best
Flesh	White
Spore colour	Pale/light brown
Smell	No distinctive smell
Habitat	Relatively open woodland (little foliage on forest floor, trees 5-10 apart) of oak, birch and beech. Likes grassy areas
Time of Year	July–October

The Hedgehog mushroom
(Hydnum repandum)

You need either to have terrible eyesight, or a severe misunderstanding of what a hedgehog is to mistake this excellent mushroom for anything else. Instead of gills (which most mushrooms have) or pores (which the *bolete* family has) on the underside of the cap, the Hedgehog mushroom has many downwards-facing spikes. The Hedgehog mushroom is quite easy to spot from a distance and then very easy to identify when close up. If you do see a Hedgehog mushroom, keep your eyes peeled for Chanterelles too as they like to grow in a similar habitat. Although the small spines have a tendency to break off when you are cooking them, they are also great at trapping the yummy bits of your sauce, especially a creamy sauce. Oooh stop it!

Cap	Cream colour, up to 10-12cm. Irregular shape. Similar in size and shape to chanterelle. Buff leather texture
Stem	Up to 6-8cm, stocky, cream
Gills	**Main distinguishing feature:** little spines instead of gills, cream colour
Flesh	Cream
Spore colour	Cream
Smell	Bitter, with a bitter taste that goes with cooking. MUST be cooked
Habitat	Woodlands, look for damp mossy areas and banks by ditches
Time of Year	August–November, can survive the first frost or two

Giant Puffball *(Calvatia gigantea)*

There is absolutely nothing that you could mistake this fungus for. Sorry, let me rephrase that. There is absolutely no other fungus that you could mistake this for. There are however, other things that could be used in a police line-up, but they're not in the least bit mushroomy. Footballs, white ducks, plastic bags... Any of these, seen from a distance, may well cause the heart to beat faster until you get close enough to see that, in fact, your giant puffball is nothing of the sort. The kid leather skin should be removed and the white, spongy flesh cut thin and fried.

Cap	**Main distinguishing feature:** usually about the size of a football or a small white duck. Same buff leather texture as hedgehog mushroom
Stem	No stem, connected to the ground by small root-like fibres
Gills	No gills
Flesh	White, anything other than white is past its best. Goes yellow/brown/green when mature
Spore colour	Brown when mature
Smell	No distinctive smell
Habitat	Mostly fields/pasture land, sometimes by the sides of paths/edges of wood
Time of Year	Summer mostly, to about September

Wood Blewit *(Lepista nuda)*

The Wood Blewit really is a solid mushroom. It has a solid stem, with chunky flesh and many neat, firm flexible gills that, due to the time of year it likes to appear, are rarely troubled by maggots. If the Wood Blewit was turning up to a party, he'd be 'fashionably late', preferring the late autumn, and is happy to hang around even after the first frosts, when many other fungi leave us for the year. The colour of this chap is nothing short of magnificent, with a vibrant lilac-purple running through the cap, stem, gills and flesh in young specimens. The Blewit also wears a rather distinctive 'perfume', that is floral and sometimes spicy – and quite addictive. Just don't let other 'non-foragers' catch you sniffing it too much. You'll get some odd looks way before you get the chance to explain. This isn't a mushroom to eat raw either. Like kidney beans, it contains a compound that makes us feel unwell if eaten uncooked, but which disappears on cooking. Good, I'm never that keen on raw mushrooms anyway. Despite having 'wood' in its name, I have never found it anywhere but in grass, though admittedly near to woods. This leads me to a great tip on where to keep your eyes peeled when you're out foraging: edges and transitions. Path edges, around car parks, the transitions between woods and grass, or even a change in tree type can all cause specific mushrooms to pop up.

Cap	Slightly translucent, 'jelly-like' outer skin to cap, up to 15cm. Flattened dome. Quite stocky, thick-set mushroom, dries paler
Stem	Up to 10cm, lilac
Gills	Lilac/purple, quite close together, flexible, looks neat
Flesh	Lilac/purple
Spore colour	Pale pink
Smell	**Main distinguishing feature:** strongly perfumed
Habitat	Variable: all types of woodland but I have only ever found them in grass, on the edge of woodland
Time of Year	September/October to December, depending on severity of frost

The Velvet Shank *(Flammulina velutipes)*

I'm assuming by the common name you've already guessed the key identification characteristic of this mushroom, and if you haven't… it's the shank… and it's velvety. But there's also another great identification point, and that is the time of year it comes out to play, long after most mushrooms have well and truly called it a day (or year). The velvet shank has a special compound that allows it to be frozen solid without destroying its cell walls, hence it can survive even the harshest of frosts. Growing in pretty clusters on dead trees or stumps, especially elm, the sticky orange-yellow caps stand out nicely. The cluster usually has a varied degree of young and old members amongst it, with the older ones tending to have darker stems that are the most velvety. Luckily, it's just the caps we eat, as the stems are tough and frankly, they look black and pretty unappetising too.

Cap	Orange that fades to pale orange, yellow at cap edge, up to 8-10cm. Can invert itself and roll backwards as it matures
Stem	Up to 6cm long, similar colour to cap when young, darkening to brown/black when older. Velvety, more pronounced when black/older
Gills	Cream to pale yellow and widely spaced
Flesh	Yellow
Spore colour	Yellow
Smell	No distinctive smell
Habitat	Grows, often in dense clusters, on dead wood stumps, mostly elm and oak
Time of Year	**Main distinguishing feature:** October–February, can survive frosts when all others have called it a day

MUSHROOMS TO STEER CLEAR OF

Although there are a number of mushrooms in this country that can make you seriously ill (or worse), I have included just two for you to remember and avoid. The first makes the list as the most deadly and the second for the frequency of its poisonings (although it won't kill you). So if you are to learn only two 'baddies', make it these two.

Death Cap *(Amanita phalloides)*

The king of deadly fungi is the Death Cap. It is the most potent of all toadstools you may come across and accounts for over 90% of fungus-related fatalities. As the name suggests, just half an adult specimen will probably see you, well, dead. I won't go into detail but rest assured that liver and kidney failure are among the ill effects. Luckily, it is difficult to mistake for any edible species (and almost impossible from my recommended mushroom list) so you should have no problems, but it is quite common so you need to know it to avoid it. The olive-green cap, droopy ring around the stem and loose volva (bag at the base of the stem that the toadstool grows from) are the key identification features.

Cap	Usually with pale olive or green tinge, smooth, flat usually quite round. Fibres radiate outwards from the centre, from 4-15cm across
Stem	White, 5-15cm long, has a droopy ring under the cap and a large, loose volva (bag at the base of the stem)
Gills	White, crowded, do not attach to stem
Flesh	White
Spore colour	White
Smell	Sickly sweet
Habitat	Small groups in mixed woodland, particularly near oak trees
Time of Year	Summer to autumn

Yellow Stainer *(Agaricus xanthodermus)*

The reason so many people get upset stomachs each year from this chap is due to its uncanny resemblance to a Field Mushroom, a species that so many of our undereducated population seem to think they know the look of and therefore assume is safe to eat. Field Mushrooms are safe, as long as they aren't Yellow Stainers that you think are Field Mushrooms! Look closely when you first pick them, as the flesh in the base of the stem (and the edge of the cap) will turn a bright yellow colour when cut/bruised. This yellow fades to brown within a few minutes so do be vigilant. If in any doubt, the smell of ink/Elastoplasts (strongest at the base of the stem) should be a giveaway, and the rather off-putting smell will intensify during cooking. If none of these clues help you to identify and avoid the Yellow Stainer, quite frankly you've earned your upset stomach through naivety!

Cap	Button mushroom shape when young, opening up to flat when older. White with pale grey/brown tinges. 5-15cm across
Stem	White, turns bright yellow at base when cut, as will the cap edge. White fragile ring under cap. 5-15cm long
Gills	White, then pink, then brown with age
Flesh	White
Spore colour	Purple/dark brown
Smell	Inky, of Elastoplasts
Habitat	Woodland edges, pastures and grass areas, including gardens
Time of Year	Summer to late autumn

PLANT FORAGING

When I first started work on this section, I had decided to keep it pretty brief for two reasons – the first being that the so-called 'abundant' plants in lots of foraging books are dubious to say the least, and secondly, well – how do I put it? – many 'recommended' plants just aren't that great to eat, so I don't want to recommend them! There is a bitterness to a lot of wild plants, which can be truly eye-watering.

Then, the more I thought about it and the more I pictured the different plants through the seasons, I realised there are quite a few that are common, easily identifiable and good to eat.

I ended up with just short of a dozen – I have assumed that you already know how to identify crab apples, dandelions, and horse chestnuts. I think we are born knowing those ones!

One key thing to bear in mind when you are foraging for leaves is to make sure to get your plant to the plate quickly (within a few hours); these leaves won't keep too well, which might surprise you if you're used to supermarket bags of salad, but then again so would the processes that the suppliers go though to get them to stay 'fresh' for so long.

Wood sorrel

In most moist, well-developed forests, this pretty little plant carpets the floor. It has three heart shaped leaves and stands about two inches tall. Very easy to identify. The flavour is incredibly punchy for a plant so small, and is likened to the sharpness/citrus flavour you get from apple peel (courtesy of oxalic acid common in the different sorrel types). It makes a seriously great addition to salads (especially exotic salads), a great edible garnish and is versatile enough to add punch when muddled in cocktails. Need I say more?

Mint/watermint

I absolutely love mint. It is so versatile and can be used in everything from sweet desserts and tummy-soothing drinks to fresh and lively Moroccan savoury classics. I have covered it in the 'grow your own' section later on, and to be honest, if it didn't smell and taste so good it, would be classed as a weed, as it grows like wildfire in a lot of environments. The mint family has three very distinctive characteristics: it has a square profile stem, leaves arranged in opposite pairs and, if you're still in any doubt, a quick rub of the leaves will release its glorious smell. Just keep your eyes peeled for this little plant around wet areas; it is a lot more common than you may have thought.

Wild garlic

There are actually quite a few plants in this country that have a 'garlic-y' flavour, and not without good reason. The chemical that the plant produces is rather good at keeping it from being eaten by animals. Unfortunately for the plants, it's the exact same compound that attracts us humans to it as a wonderful addition to nearly every savoury meal. The two best types to forage for are Ramsons and Three Cornered Garlic. Ramsons can fill a glade in a shaded woodland from March to June, no problem at all, so finding and picking enough for a meal is a doddle. Three Cornered Garlic is just that, having a distinctive triangular profile to its long, thin stems. It is mainly found in road verges and hedgerows. Its white flowers are similar in shape to bluebells, and come out prolifically at about the same time, and are a pleasure to see in the spring. The flowers are edible and, to be honest, the best bit, having a deliciously sweet, firm crunch with a mild garlic flavour. They look and taste great as a foraged topping or garnish to almost any meal. (See our Wild Garlic and Watercress Spanish Omelette Recipe on page 172)

Sloes

Another hedgerow find, sloes (the berry of the blackthorn) are very easy to identify. They first come out in late August/early September and although traditionally sloes should not be picked until after the first frosts, as the freezing process begins to break down the sugars and improves the flavour of the fruit, there is a great tip to 'ripening' them yourself. You can artificially recreate these frosts by placing your picked sloes in the freezer overnight. Ordinarily I wouldn't advocate making sloe gin and drinking it in the same year. I believe the longer it is left to ferment the better. However a long wait can be quite tough on your first ever sloe gin attempt, so try the overnight freezing trick at the end of August and then at least your brew will be a few months old by the time Christmas comes around. Experiment a little, too; try adding other flavours like honey instead of some of the sugar, and the rind of a large orange will give a citrus punch that can cut through the rather sweet flavour beautifully.

Here is my very simple Sloe Gin recipe: take 400-500g of sloes and prick them with a fork or knife. Take the same amount of sugar and 600mls of gin (the cheap stuff will do fine), throw it all in a bottle, shake hard and store your bottle in a cool dark place. Then, turn the bottle every day for a week, then every week for a month or two. Ideally, you should allow it to ferment for longer than three months (please do), and when ready to drink, strain the fruit and re-bottle.

Elderflower

If you are only going to learn to identify one plant from this list, be sure that it's the elderflower. Why? Well, you get the most bang for your buck. The elder tree can produce three – yes, three – excellent harvests. The trees are easiest to spot between May and July, as the white-cream flower heads (they can grow to the size of a small side plate) will be dotted all over the tree and make them stand out a mile. In the autumn come the berries, and, finally, you get 'jelly ear' fungi that grow almost exclusively on dead elder branches. The flower heads are totally amazing, but be quick, as the window of opportunity to pick them when ripe is quite small, lasting only a few weeks. Check out our elderflower cordial recipe, (on page 174), which you can then go on to include in the Gin Garden cocktail and wow your friends with throughout the summer. The flower heads can be dried to make them last longer, but if you do pick all the flowers, don't expect any berries that year, as the tree won't produce any without them. The berries again lend themselves to drinks rather well, and if you're feeling more ambitious, you can find a recipe for your own elderberry wine or a simple juice on the internet, that will be delicious. As for the Jelly Ear fungus, I would say that it has an 'interesting texture' and leave it at that. If you're interested, you can find out for yourself!

Wall Pennywort

You'll ideally find this on moss-covered walls – it loves a damp environment to grow on. Not actually recommended very much, as people tend to think it has a bland flavor We couldn't disagree more, and with all the oriental cooking Trevor does, this crunchy beansprout-flavoured freebie is an awesome addition. And the best bit? There is never that hint of bitterness that so many other wild plants seem to have. The disc-shaped leaves are thick, crunchy and juicy, and are unmistakable, growing in small clusters out of old rocky walls or shady, moist banks. Only throw them in the dish at the last minute or they will lose their bite.

Stinging Nettles

I sincerely hope these need no introduction, or even any identification tips. Mix water and baking soda into a paste and apply to the skin if you get stung by them! Always try picking the tips (top 6-8 leaves) of the nettle. Like many wild plants, the older leaves tend to have a bitterness about them. I would suggest picking with rubber gloves on to avoid getting stung. When boiled, they can make a delicious soup (and the stinging mechanism is broken down when they are boiled) or be added to a risotto – see our recipe on page 170.

Marsh & Rock Samphire

Marsh samphire is nice but a bit scarce, while rock samphire is not so nice but is everywhere. Sometimes that's just how nature rolls. Marsh samphire is good – no, great – and I'm sure at some point you will have seen it on the menu at some posh restaurants. It's a crunchy, succulent plant with a salty flavour that works well as a steamed bed on which to lay a beautiful, firm piece of grilled fresh fish. My mouth is watering at the very thought of it! It is not hugely abundant but look out for any firm, flat, sheltered muddy/sandy areas that are exposed when the tide is out and only just covered when it's in – i.e. marine marshy areas, hence the name. (See our recipe for Grass-cooked Trout with Marsh samphire on page 231.) Rock samphire has a strong taste like citronella, and if you get a hint of turpentine you are spot on. It doesn't just taste of turpentine, it is turpentine – it contains pinene, a major constituent of turpentine – but it's perfectly safe to eat. It is best pickled to try and mask the flavour, and if I'm honest it only made it on this list because it is so common, and to differentiate it from marsh samphire. Otherwise, it should be left where it is, unless you're in a survival situation.

Fat Hen

This plant's leaves are a great addition to salads. It is most notably found on wasteland, in particular the unused areas of allotments! People try so hard to grow great spinach and lettuces, and Fat Hen is often removed from their plot as a weed. The irony! Quite distinctive in appearance, with triangular/spear-shaped leaves, with the newer leaves in particular covered in what looks like a dusting of flour. Succulent and tasty with rarely any bitterness to it, this is a firm favourite of ours.

Alexanders

Quite an acquired taste (don't say I didn't warn you); very aromatic with a strong celery flavour. It is the stems we are interested in, which take a similar form to celery sticks. Don't eat them past Easter, as they become very woody and fibrous, to the point where your favourite kitchen knife might well become blunt. Stick to the earlier shoots that are much more tender. Introduced by the Romans, Alexanders are very common and although not a true marine plant, are virtually always within a couple of miles of the shoreline, seriously dominating road verges with their tall stems (up to 1.2 metres in height) and their distinctive yellow flowers in spring. If you know what cow parsley looks like, Alexanders are almost the same but with yellow flower heads instead of white. Give them a try and see what you think – Trevor suggests a modern forager's take on the traditional mussels in celery and wine, choosing Alexanders and cider instead!

Pig Nuts

I've included these because of the pure fun you can have in finding them, which transports me straight back to being five years old and digging in the mud for worms. It's not actually a nut though; it's a tuber (like a potato) that is grown by the plant as an underground energy store. You identify the pig nut by its flowers and leaves that grow above ground. You can eat them raw, straight out of the ground and they have a lovely crunchy texture and flavour, just like a nut. Roasted whole, they will taste very similar to horse chestnuts. Also check out the pig nut pesto recipe, on page 178 where the pig nuts replace pine nuts. It could take you a while to gather enough for a small bowlful, so that's why we recommend making something out of them like pesto where a little goes a long way.

NETTLE RISOTTO WITH ROASTED BUTTERNUT SQUASH AND WALNUTS

NETTLES ARE A GOOD source of vitamins and minerals and are probably the easiest plant to identify, so you shouldn't have a problem locating your quarry.

Place the squash wedges on a roasting tray, along with the garlic cloves, a good drizzle of olive oil, sea salt and pepper. Roast in the oven for 40-50 minutes until softened and golden. Add the walnuts after 30 minutes, checking to make sure they don't burn.

Blanch the nettles in boiling salted water for two minutes, then drain, squeeze dry, and chop finely. Wash and chop the wild garlic leaves.

Melt the butter in a heavy-based saucepan and sweat the onion in this liquid for a few minutes until softened. Add the rice, coating it in the liquid in the pan and cook for a further few minutes. Add the wine, stirring constantly until all the liquid has been absorbed.

Add a ladle of the hot stock and allow the rice to absorb the liquid. The mix should come to a gentle simmer.

Keep adding the stock, one ladle at a time, until the liquid is all absorbed, the risotto is creamy, and the rice still has a little bite (*al dente*). You should keep stirring throughout, to make sure the risotto does not catch on the bottom of the pan.

Stir the chopped nettles and garlic leaves into the risotto. Season to taste with salt and pepper.

Cut the roasted squash into smaller cubes. Serve the risotto with a generous heap of squash and walnuts and a trickle of olive oil on each portion.

[SERVES FOUR]

1 BUTTERNUT SQUASH, PEELED
 AND CUT IN HALF
 LENGTHWAYS, AND THEN
 AGAIN INTO 6-8 WEDGES
A HANDFUL OF WALNUTS
OLIVE OIL
2 GARLIC CLOVES, PEELED
30-40 NETTLE TOPS
SMALL BUNCH OF WILD GARLIC
 LEAVES
1 LARGE ONION, FINELY
 CHOPPED
75G BUTTER
400G ARBORIO RICE
1L CHICKEN OR VEGETABLE
 STOCK
250ML WHITE WINE
SEA SALT AND FRESHLY GROUND
 BLACK PEPPER

WILD GARLIC AND WATERCRESS SPANISH OMELETTE

- -

AN EASY SUPPER DISH, that always goes down well. You will need a 9-inch frying pan for this recipe.

Dice the potatoes into 10mm cubes and par boil for 4-5 minutes.

Whisk the eggs in a large bowl.

Trim the dandelion petals off the head using scissors and add to the whisked eggs, along with salt and pepper.

Finely chop the onion and bell pepper, and gently fry in a 9-inch frying pan with some olive oil.

Drain the par-boiled potatoes and add to the pan and fry for 2-3 minutes.

Add the chopped wild garlic and watercress to the pan for 30 seconds before pouring the whisked egg and dandelion petal mix over the onion, pepper and potatoes, and turn the heat to low. Cook until there is virtually no liquid egg left on the top of the omelette.

Run a knife around the edge of the pan to loosen it, and then place a plate or lid over the pan, and flip. Now slide your omelette back into the pan.

Sprinkle grated cheese (optional) on top and place your pan under a medium grill to brown.

Serve hot or cold with a green salad, a good Spanish wine and friends in the warm summer sunshine.

[SERVES FOUR]

6 LARGE FREE RANGE EGGS
10 NEW POTATOES, APPROX.
   500G
3 HANDFULS OF WATERCRESS
3 HANDFULS (TREVOR-SIZE
HANDFULS I.E. LARGE!) OF WILD
   GARLIC OR RAMSONS LEAVES
1 MEDIUM ONION
1 RED BELL PEPPER
PETALS OF 2 DANDELION HEADS
SALT AND PEPPER
OLIVE OIL FOR FRYING
CHEDDAR OR TETILLA (A MILD
   MELTING SPANISH CHEESE)
   OPTIONAL

ELDERFLOWER CORDIAL

IN LATE MAY TO EARLY JUNE, up and down the country, small trees with yellow bark are covered by large, dense florets made up of tiny white flowers. The flowers have a delicious sweet smell to them and, not only do they smell good, they also taste good as well. The flowers are elderflowers and they have been used as food and for medicinal purposes for years.

In Stroud where I grew up, there is a company that makes elderflower cordial and in the summer months they used to pay for elderflowers collected by locals. My friends and I used to scour the valleys for elderflower trees and strip them of their flowers; this often meant wading through head-high stinging nettles and climbing up thin fragile branches. Eventually we would get to the bottling plant with our plastic bags full of elderflowers to have them weighed and to collect our prize. It was a good job that I was young and poor back then, because the going rate was £1 for 1lb. If you weigh how much you have collected in an afternoon, you'll see that that's a lot of effort for fairly little reward. We used to try and make the flowers heavier by spraying water on them but you had to be careful because if you were caught, they wouldn't take your flowers. The locals used to make quite a mess of the countryside in the search for elderflowers and the company decided to stop this practice, and instead harvest their own, which was probably good news for Stroud.

Dissolve the sugar in boiling water in a large pan, then allow to cool completely. Slice lemons and add to elderflower heads (with leaves and large stalks removed) in another large pan and cover with citric acid. Pour over dissolved sugar/syrup mix, place lid on and leave (minimum 8 hours) overnight to infuse. Strain the whole lot through a fine meshed sieve into a jug or other container with a pouring lip. Now pour the cordial into clean sterilised bottles for storage and freeze some for later use.

To serve, put cordial into a glass and top up with still or sparkling water and ice cubes for an amazingly refreshing, home-made summer drink.

Our top tip is to make the syrup before collecting flower heads as it takes several hours to fully cool and the best flavour is achieved from the freshest elderflowers. Citric acid is not always easy to get hold of but is essential; try wine-making shops, health food stores, chemists, or try the internet. The syrup is super-sticky and seems to get everywhere!

[WILL MAKE TWO LITRES OF CORDIAL]

WATER, 1.5L
SUGAR, 1.5 KG
ELDERFLOWER HEADS, MIN 25 LARGE HEADS
CITRIC ACID, 50G
LEMONS, 3 SMALL/ 2 LARGE

THE GIN GARDEN

LASTLY, FOR THOSE OF YOU who are 'of age', you must try a cocktail called a Gin Garden. It is, in our not-so-humble opinion, the quintessential British summer drink.

Peel and cut the cucumber into one inch chunks and roughly mash. Pour all of your ingredients plus the cucumber preferably into a cocktail shaker. Add ice and shake for 30-60 seconds. (If you don't have a shaker, a large glass with something over the top will do!) Strain through a fine sieve (to remove cucumber lumps) into a chilled glass and enjoy!

[FOR ONE COCKTAIL]

1 1/2 SHOTS GIN
1 SHOT ELDERFLOWER CORDIAL
1/3 OF A PEELED CUCUMBER
1/4 FRESH LEMON, SQUEEZED
1 SHOT PRESSED APPLE JUICE
   (PREFERABLY COPELLA)

PIG NUT PESTO

I got this recipe from John Wright, a man who taught us practically everything we know about foraging. So if you try this and like it, you have him to thank. If you want to know more about John and his amazing foraging courses, go to **http:// www.wild-food.net/**

Now, to the recipe. It will make one small jar, although pesto goes a long way as the flavour is so intense.

Blitz everything but the oil in a food processor until finely chopped, then slowly stir in the oil, little by little. And that's it.

Admittedly, it takes a while to collect 30-40g of pig nuts but I know of no better way to enjoy them than this simple pig nut pesto tossed into fresh spaghetti. Add a dollop of crème fraîche or sour cream for a smoother, less intense flavour.

30-40G PIG NUTS, SLICED AND
  BRIEFLY ROASTED IN A LITTLE
  OIL
30G PARMESAN CHEESE, FINELY
  GRATED
50G WILD GARLIC LEAVES
80ML OLIVE OIL
SALT AND PEPPER

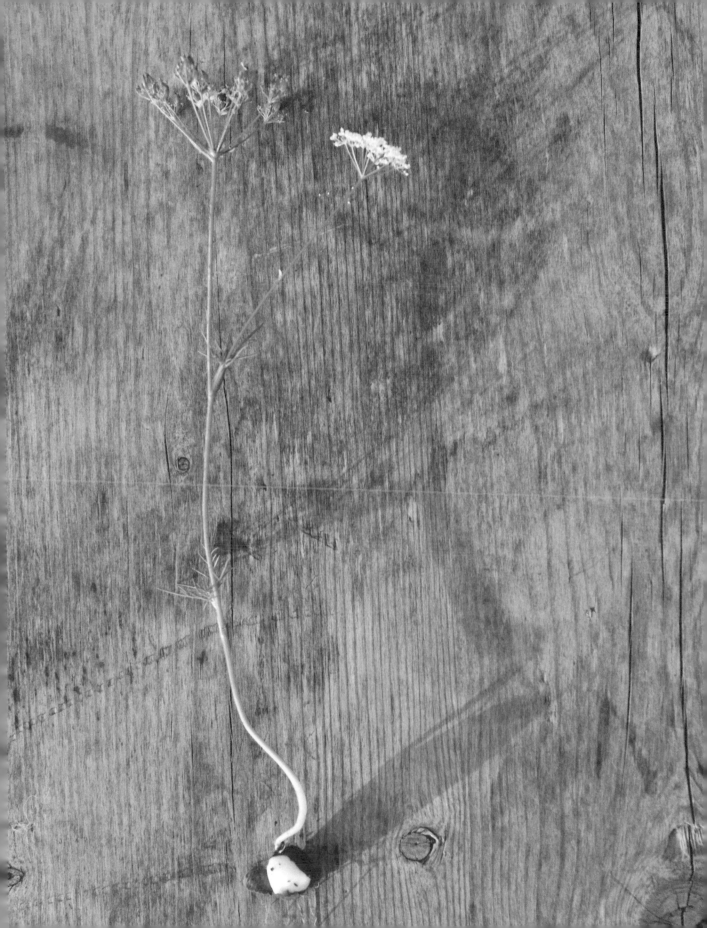

GUNS AND SHOOTING

ONE WAY TO PROVIDE for the pot when out in woods and fields is, of course, with the help of a gun – rabbits, pheasants, roe deer and much more, can make wonderful food to eat. But as with many activities, this requires knowledge of the law and a sensible attitude to safety before embarking on a day out with a gun.

THE LAW

There are three types of guns mainly used for hunting in the UK: shotguns, hunting rifles and air rifles. The first two are over the legal limit of 12ft lbs of pressure, which means that to own one of these, you will need a firearms licence, only available through your local constabulary. Go to **http://www.met.police.uk/firearms_licensing/** for more information.

And remember, you should never use a gun on public land. If you do, expect the armed police squad to turn up. If anyone reports the sighting of a gun of any description in use in a public place, the police will arrive in a matter of minutes. Always stick to private land, and if it's not your own land, make sure you have the landowner's permission. Rules, rules, rules I know, but they are there for everyone's safety.

TYPES OF GUN

1. Shotguns

These come in various sizes, and fire multiple ball bearings. They are great for clay pigeon shooting as well as hunting rabbits, pheasant, duck and pretty much all game. A Section 2 Firearms Licence is required to own and harbour one.

2. Hunting rifles

These fire what you would traditionally think of as a bullet, and are powerful enough to kill a deer stone dead at 300m with an accurate shot. Very useful I hear you say, but unless you shoot a lot, it's not worth the bother. Section 1 Firearms Licence is required to own and harbour one.

3. Air rifles

These are the ones to go for if you're either starting out or don't plan on doing much shooting. Unlike the two examples above, they require no Firearms Licence if their power limit is up to 12ft lbs. Any more and a licence would be needed, any less and you will struggle to kill your required targets i.e. rabbits, birds etc. This is the power limit you should be searching for.

Air rifles come in two main sizes, relating to their barrel and pellet diameter: 0.177 or 0.22 (of an inch) with the smaller sizes better for hitting small vermin at distances of up to 35 metres, and the bigger sizes better in windy conditions or over shorter distances. Again, two main firing mechanisms are common in air rifles, spring loaded and gas powered (by CO2). Spring loaded work by compressing a spring that is released when the trigger is fired and this spring forces air through the barrel, propelling the pellet in front of it. They are cheaper, but you can only fire once before needing to re-load and they have much more 'recoil' (kick back) than gas-powered air rifles. Gas-powered air rifles are more expensive but have very little recoil and can be bought with multi-shot (up to 8 without reloading the pellet or gas) mechanisms. They are usually good for about 40 shots before the CO2 canister needs topping up, so they do have higher running costs too.

DON'T ever point a gun, loaded or not, at a person. This is the number one rule.

DON'T shoot animals for fun. Only shoot what you intend to eat, or as pest control.

DO buy the best pellets you can afford. Better quality pellets fly straighter and are much more accurate over longer distances.

DON'T attempt to shoot anything out of killing distance (about 35m) as you may hit but not kill instantly, allowing the animal to run away but suffer.

DO take time to accurately sight your scope.

DO always go for a head shot for an instant kill.

DO respect your gun, paying attention to cleaning and maintenance.

DO get the landowner's permission before stepping on to any property. It is illegal to shoot on someone else's property, so always make sure you have full permission.

DO practise using targets to improve your aim.

TIPS ON SETTING UP A SCOPE FOR A RIFLE

A good quality scope, sighted correctly is just as important as the gun. To accurately sight your scope follow these tips:

1.

Mount your scope firmly on the gun or get a local gunsmith to do it for you. The eye piece should be 2-4 inches from your eye when holding the gun naturally in the shoulder in firing position. The scope has two dials, one for adjusting up and down (this should be on the top of the scope when fitted) and the other for adjusting left and right (this should be on the right).

2.

It is helpful to have a vice style table, like a work bench, to secure the gun steadily while 'tuning' or 'zeroing' the scope. If not, just make sure you have some sort of structure to lean on that will enable you to make repeated stable shots.

3.

Set your target at a distance you will most often be shooting your animal at. The max killing distance on a 12ft lbs air rifle is about 35m, so tuning the scope at a target 25-30m distance is about right.

4.

Now the fun bit! Holding the gun steadily against a firm structure and taking your time, line the 'crosshair' in the scope with the target and shoot. If you hit the bull's-eye first time it will be luck! Take 3-5 shots, always aiming the crosshair at the centre of the target. You should notice a fairly consistent 'grouping' of holes in the target. Adjust the dials up or down, left or right depending on where the grouping lands and then try another 3-5 shots. Keep adjusting until your grouping is as close to the centre as possible.

5.

Then go shoot them pesky wabbits, as Elmer Fudd would say.

Shooting Rabbits

Every summer holidays when I was a nipper, I would head 'ooop north' to my grandparent's farm in Lancashire to generally cause a nuisance for a week with my brother and cousins. Looking back, this was clearly where my love for the countryside was born.

We used to go down the 'bottom side', the bit of the farm where we could climb trees and splash around in the stream, which depending on recent rain, would vary from a small trickle to quite a flowing little river. Then, after a few hours, we would return home, wet, muddy and tired but with huge smiles on our faces. Depending on the time of year, we would also have the chance to get involved in either mushroom picking, lambing or helping with (well, building dens in amongst) the huge delivery of hay bales. On return to the farmhouse, the teapot, almost constantly in use, would be ready on the Aga and before long we would be warm, dry and well fed, thanks to the efforts of my incredible granny. Man, she knows how to cook!

These childish activities went on happily for a few years until – and I still remember the moment – my dad decided I was now old enough and wise enough to go out rabbit shooting. I had spent many years watching the 'adults' get kitted up with wellies, Barbours, shotguns and cartridge belts to head out into the woods, as the late afternoon sun dipped, hearing for the hundredth time the dreaded phrase for any young 'un... 'You're just not old enough yet'... In the year or two before this fateful day, I had been out once or twice with my father and brother (without a gun, of course) so that I was familiar with all the gun safety procedures.

So, my father and I headed out, and to cut a long story short, I came home with a lovely brace of rabbits on my very first outing (Dad didn't get any that night!) I was absolutely beaming with pride that I was the hunter bringing home the dinner. I hadn't, however, fully considered the next stage. My uncle George, who ran the farm, looked at me and said, 'You know how to skin them, right?'. With what I imagine to be quite a worried look on my face, I said no, hoping that he would take pity and do the skinning for me. Shooting them was one thing, but pulling the skin off and the guts out was entirely another! He made me an offer: he would show me how to do the first one and I would have to do the second.

So here is the method I learnt many moons ago, which has not changed much since. Incidentally we ate the rabbits the next night in a casserole that my granny showed me. It was amazing – if I do say so myself – so I've included the recipe for a classic game casserole too.

HOW TO SKIN A RABBIT

ALWAYS SKIN A RABBIT with an adult if you are under 16.

Skinning a rabbit is not for the faint-hearted, especially if it's still warm and you have, as I did the first time I tried, both pangs of guilt and thoughts of my dear cat, Bruno, who was a similar size, shape and texture. My advice is to take a deep breath and roll your sleeves up, or you'll look like a girl. It may initially seem like a long and messy process, but a whole rabbit can be gutted and skinned in about a minute and a half once you get good at it.

WHAT YOU'LL NEED:
plenty of newspaper,
a large, sturdy chopping board,
a short-bladed, very sharp knife,
meat cleaver or a small hacksaw.

Step 1.

With the rabbit on its back, 'unzip' the belly by cutting from between the back legs up to under the chin. This can be done in two steps when you're a beginner, firstly splitting the fur exposing the skin, then opening the skin. Be very, very, very careful when cutting the skin that you don't insert the knife too far, piercing the gut. The guts don't look great and they definitely don't smell any better. Use a gentle steady motion only inserting the knife tip by 5-10mm.

Step 2.

Hold the rabbit up by its front legs, letting the back legs hang down. Hold it over newspaper or a plastic bag to catch the guts and using two fingers (middle and index) insert into the cavity, grasping the inside of the throat area and pulling down to disconnect the guts. Once you have disconnected these from the throat area, all the guts will fall out, leaving you with an empty body cavity. The only things left behind should be the kidneys, two small red balls attached either side of the spine. Remove them if you want to.

Step 3.

Using either a meat cleaver or a small hacksaw, cut off the head and each of the legs. Cut about 2/3rds of the legs off as there is little meat on this part and it makes skinning so much easier. Then, starting with the back legs, manoeuvre the skin off the bone, a little like taking an arm out of a jacket sleeve. Do this with both back legs, taking the skin off in one piece down to the rib cage. Then get a firm hold of the back legs in one hand and the skin in the other and pull with a strong steady motion. The skin should come off the rest of the rabbit, in one piece.

You are now left with meat on the carcass in the rear legs and the front shoulders. The best use of this meat is to boil it and then flake it off the bone. However you must cook for 2 to $2\frac{1}{2}$ hours or the meat will be incredibly tough. After two and a half hours it should be soft and fall off the bone. Then add the meat to any dish you like. Or, read Trevor's recipe for a delicious rabbit stew opposite.

RABBIT STEW

NOW THAT YOU HAVE successfully skinned your rabbit, give this recipe a go to make a delicious and filling stew. Depending on how old the rabbit is it may need to be cooked for longer, as older rabbits tend to be tougher than younger ones. If in doubt, try a bit of the meat; it should be tender and easy to pull from the bone. If you are using more than one rabbit, try to ensure they are the same age. If they aren't, cook the older rabbit for longer than the younger rabbit.

Coat the rabbit joints in seasoned flour. Next, melt the butter in a casserole pan or other heavy bottomed pan and brown the floured rabbit joints. Once they are nicely browned all over, add the stock, wine, bouquet garni and tomato puree to the pot and bring to the boil. Crush the garlic and add to the pan. Season to taste.

Reduce the heat and simmer for 2 hours or until the rabbit meat is tender and comes away from the bone easily. Remove the rabbit joints and set aside.

Add the cornflour and double cream to the pan to thicken the sauce. Season to taste, then pour over rabbit joints and serve.

[FOR SIX]

2KG JOINTED RABBIT
300ML CHICKEN OR VEGETABLE
    STOCK
2 TBSP SEASONED FLOUR
2 TSP TOMATO PUREE
2 CLOVES OF GARLIC
150ML WHITE WINE
BOUQUET GARNI – lots of herbs
    tied together. Try 1 bay leaf, 3
    sprigs of thyme, 2 sticks of
    celery, 3 sprigs of parsley.
2 TSP CORNFLOUR
50G BUTTER
2 TBSP DOUBLE CREAM

5. URBAN

GROWING YOUR OWN

'GROWING YOUR OWN' can vary from simply having a few herbs on the windowsill to a full-on allotment. If you do have a bit of spare time (you will be surprised how much time it can take) and fancy an allotment, you will need to contact your local council – be warned though, most have quite a lengthy waiting list. Your second best option is to sign up to the brilliant Landshare scheme, which connects people with land to those who want some, in order to grow vegetables. **(http://www.landshare.net/)**

The Three Hungry Boys like working smart, as opposed to working hard, and even though we are short of space, we have adapted our concrete backyard to accommodate a few great plants that require the minimum effort. Just because we live in the city doesn't mean we can't live the good life too. We simply knocked up a raised bed out of a couple of old railway sleepers, filled the bottom with a few inches of pebbles and shingle to help with drainage, and then topped it up with about a foot of regular earth and compost. Don't worry about tools too much either – we use a pair of scissors to cut things off and an old bricklaying trowel for planting or moving soil about, and that's it.

All you have to do when growing your own is to remember the two golden rules:

1.

Pick an area that gets a good amount of direct sunlight. Whether you are growing herbs on the windowsill, building a raised bed or you've got a pitch at an allotment, the fundamental point is that plants need sunlight to grow. So make sure they get plenty of it.

2.

Keep your plants well watered. The shallower your soil, the quicker it will dry out, especially in warm areas, so windowsills will need watering every 24-48 hours, while your allotment may only need it once a week, even in hot weather.

WHAT TO GROW

If you are new to the growing game, I would suggest choosing a plant which will give you the most 'bang for your buck'. I also urge you to thoroughly investigate the foraging section of our Woods and Fields chapter. Each plant that you eventually choose to grow will have originated from a wild plant, and what's the point of growing your own spinach or rocket, if the wild plant (or a closely related one) grows abundantly in your area? I learnt this lesson after spending £7 on a raspberry plant that, if I'm honest, gives me very little fruit, only to discover more raspberries than I could possibly eat surrounding my local cricket pitch.

So here's a few tips and suggestions for growing your own, but I must stress you really should grow what you want to.

Herbs in the windowsill

I recommend growing every plant from seeds, except herbs. I don't know why, but we can never get them to grow big and strong. So we just buy and replant a small plant from the supermarket or greengrocer – oregano, thyme or basil are great for cooking – or grow from cuttings from an established plant, like rosemary, that we just happen to come across. If you do try growing herbs from seeds, hopefully you'll have better luck than us!

KEY POINTS: Starting seeds on a warm and sunny windowsill gives plants a great start. Grow them for a month or two before transferring to bigger pots or direct into the ground.

GROW RATING: Easy

Beetroot

Tim loves beetroot. I always used to hate it as a child because it turned my favourite salad item – cucumber – bright purple. But as a result of his enthusiasm, I have grown to love it too, and when we grew our own, we discovered that beetroot is awesome in more ways than one. First, it gives the bright purple root that is great to eat when cooked. Second, its leaves are not only edible, but deliciously so.

KEY POINTS: Plant seeds indoors in March, direct outdoors from April/May and harvest three months later. The roots should be up to a tennis ball size if conditions have been perfect but even a small ping-pong size ball will taste great. The leaves are delicious in a salad.

GROW RATING: Medium

Chilli Peppers

If we're talking bang for your buck, chillies will deliver a good volume of produce per plant, and, as we all know, their flavour and heat is pretty punchy for their size too! Fairly easy to grow, but definitely start them off on your windowsill. Only move them outside in a good summer.

KEY POINTS: Hates the wet and cold, loves the sun and warmth. Plant in March indoors, harvest in August. Water occasionally.

GROW RATING: Easy

Tomatoes

Wisdom is knowing that a tomato is a fruit; common sense is knowing not to put it in a fruit salad. Home grown tomatoes are – hang on a sec. while I work this out on my calculator – precisely one million times better (and more satisfying) than their pale, shop-bought cousins. As soon as the first hard, green tomatoes appear, you will be willing them on so much that by the time they are ready to pick, I doubt they will even make it back to the kitchen. Just chop them up with a couple of fresh basil leaves, a lug of olive oil and some black pepper, and you will soon understand the joys of growing your own produce.

KEY POINTS: Plant seeds indoors in March, transfer to bigger pots/outdoors when 15-20cm tall (about May), harvest in July–September when deep red and plump. Tomato 'feeds' (liquid nutrients) are widely available and boost production. Following dry conditions with heavy watering leads to split fruit so little and often is best.

GROW RATING: Medium/Easy

Mint

In Greek mythology, Minthe was the mistress of Hades, King of the Underworld. Hades' wife Persephone took offence on discovering this and cast a spell, transforming her into a lowly weed to be trampled upon. Hades showed mercy on Minthe, and endowed her with a sweet, divine scent that she emitted every time she was trampled on to remind him of the love they shared. Hence our sweet-smelling mint today! Cultivating mint is very easy in our opinion, so it's our best bet if you want an easy ride to Successville.

KEY POINTS: Sun or shade, mint will grow. Just make sure it is kept separate in pots or it will invade the rest of your patch. Likes moist soil and has an almost year-round growth.

GROW RATING: Virtually impossible to kill. V. easy!

Salads – spinach/lettuces/chard

We highly recommend planting some sort of edible salad leaves, and varieties that come under the 'cut and come again' category are great. Not only do they grow quickly, repeatedly giving you a crop of something to eat, but their rapid growth also encourages you to collect your bounty regularly, forcing you to visit your patch and tend to your other crops.

KEY POINTS: For lettuce, start indoors at any time; stagger planting seeds so you have crops over longer time periods; grow outdoors from April to September, cut and come again (cut three inches above ground level, it will grow back in two to four weeks). Avoid very hot conditions in summer or the leaves will taste bitter. Slugs and snails may be a problem – see our Beer Tent on page 192 to counteract.

GROW RATING: Medium/Easy

The Three Sisters

Sweetcorn, a climbing legume (peas or French beans) and a cucurbit (squash, pumpkin or courgette) is a classic combination to plant together, as they have features that complement each other, creating a sort of cultivators' harmony. Plant the sweetcorn first, which will grow quickly and provide a strong frame for the climbing legume, planted two weeks after, to grow up. The legume will feed nitrogen back into the soil, spurting the growth of the cucurbit and sweetcorn, and the cucurbit (plant two weeks after the legume) will have plenty of bushy leaves at low level, keeping the soil cool and moist and crowding out any weeds.

KEY POINTS: Corn: sow seed direct to soil in May, water well after flowering, harvest August/September. Legume (pea): plant two weeks after corn, add compost but avoid manure, harvest after two to three months. Cucurbit (squash): plant seed two weeks after the legume. If the weather is wet for a few days, pick or place something between the damp soil and the fruit to prevent rotting.

GROW RATING: Medium

WHERE TO GROW YOUR OWN

Here are some handy tips on where to grow your plants:

Rows of guttering on a sunny wall for seedlings

This is one of the greatest ideas for home cultivation you will ever come across. It has so many benefits. The rounded shape allows just the right amount of compost to start seeds off and to grow to a sturdy size. You can easily cut the guttering to fit in your windowsill, and the black plastic retains heat perfectly, helping the small seeds to get growing as quickly as possible. When your plant has grown enough to go outside, it is an absolute doddle to dig a trench in a raised bed and literally slide the plants out of the guttering in one move. Perfect!

A makeshift 'greenhouse'

A little while ago, when Tim and I were refitting the bathroom at home, we just so happened to be building a large raised bed in our backyard, as our windowsill was getting a bit overcrowded. Just before we made a journey to the tip, Tim came up with the idea of using our old hinged shower screen to make a sort of greenhouse over our vulnerable raised bed seedlings. So we simply screwed the screen into the wall to create a warm, protected area that our plants now thrive in. So the moral is: keep your eyes peeled. You never know when something you thought was junk might turn out to be perfect for another purpose.

Growing potatoes in car tyres.

If like us, you struggle for space in a small back garden that has more concrete than earth, a great way to grow root vegetables such as potatoes, carrots or parsnips is to use some old car tyres as a growing receptacle. Stack two or three tyres of the same diameter on top of each other, creating a tower, and fill the central space with earth/compost. Using a drill and/or a jig saw, cut out five holes the size of a tennis ball, equally spaced apart, around the tread of each tyre. Now all you have to do is push your 'seed' potatoes in – one in each hole – about an inch or two deep, water the whole lot from the top and wait for the plants to sprout green shoots and leaves out of each little 'hole'! Gives a great harvest for taking up just a small area.

GROW RATING: Easy

PEST CONTROL

Here are our two favourite ways of keeping intruders out of your patch

1. Marigolds

There are quite a few different plants that, if grown as companions, help to keep pests away, and the most famous of these is the humble marigold. Not only will marigolds brighten up a dull vegetable patch, but the smell from the flowers deters quite a few different flying invaders, and the roots produce a chemical which keeps slugs and nematodes away, leaving you (hopefully) with a pest-free crop. Plant them in a ring surrounding your patch and they will get to work instantly as border security.

2. Beer tent for slugs

Cut a plastic bottle in half about five inches up from the bottom. Bury it in the ground so that 10mm protrudes above the soil. Slugs are quite partial to beer, and like the Three Hungry Boys, it can lead to their downfall. Fill the bottle bottom almost to the top with a mixture of half water, half lager. Slugs are lightweights and it doesn't take much to get them drunk. If it's undiluted, they won't drink it and if it's too weak they'll just have a free beer, at your expense, then head home legless (bad pun). Now make a little pitched roof (like a tent) over your slug swimming pool using wood, plastic, or whatever you have to hand. The aim is to create a warm, dark, moist area where slugs and snails will like to hang out – and the roof will also stop your beer from evaporating too quickly. If you can't bear to waste good beer, milk works too but when it goes off, it can smell pretty bad. Check on your beer tent every three or four days, to empty it of slugs and replenish the beer if necessary.

COMPOSTING

You know all those bits of leftover food you throw in the bin? I'm talking about the eggshells and toast crusts from breakfast and that salad that you just couldn't finish, even though you had a large slice of chocolate cake for pudding. Well, rather than confining them to the bin, all of those tasty morsels can instead be used to produce a rich, nutritious compost which will guarantee that your vegetables and flowers will grow big and strong.

Composting is really simple and requires the absolute minimum of effort; after all, a compost heap is really just a pile where you throw things; the worms and bacteria take care of the rest.

To get started you just need a patch of land that you can dedicate to the compost heap. Most people use a bin or composter but there is nothing stopping you from just throwing your grass and leftovers onto the patch and going from there. Having said that, composting works faster with heat and the more compact you keep your heap, the hotter it gets, so, if possible, it is best to use a bin to make your compost in.

To start things off, it is a good idea to mix grass cuttings with some chipped wood or woody matter. This gives you an excellent foundation to work with. Once you have a good base, just start piling your other bits of food and matter on, as and when you have them. You'll probably find that your pile shrinks as things begin to break down and get eaten by worms and bugs; this is normal and a sign that the decomposing process is well under way. The compost is ready when it looks dark brown and smells earthy. It is a good idea to start one pile, get it to a good size and then start a second pile next to it, so that the first pile is left to get on with its business without being disrupted by having fresh matter put on top of it.

That really is all there is to it, and if you follow these simple guidelines you'll be well on the way to creating a glorious heap of compost that will make you the envy of gardeners for miles around.

WHAT CAN BE COMPOSTED:

1.

As a rule of thumb, anything that comes from a living thing can be composted. For the purpose of composting, these can be divided into 'green' and 'brown' materials. 'Green' materials are high in nitrogen and 'brown' materials are high in carbon. Green materials are things like grass cuttings, tea bags, vegetable peel, garden weeds and manure. Brown materials are things like cardboard, wood, old plants and bedding from pets. To make really good compost, you'll want a 50:50 mix of both.

2.

Try to avoid putting cooked food or meat in the compost; they tend to rot and smell and will also attract vermin.

3.

Composting can take up to a year sometimes. You can help it along by mixing it up every now and again, and making sure that it doesn't get too dry. If this happens, add some water or moist matter to help things along.

LES ESCARGOTS – AKA SNAILS

IN THE GARDEN, SNAILS are a pain. This year alone, these pesky molluscs have grazed their way happily through half of our bean plants, a fair amount of our spinach and have made a good start on our raspberry leaves. Traps have had a bit of success, but we're loath to use slug pellets as we don't want the chemicals to leach into our soil and potentially get into the food itself. So a new solution is needed. It turns out that the species of snails that happily graze on my garden (*Helix aspersa*) are perfectly edible and are, in fact, one of the species of snails that the French so love to chomp as *les escargots*. A buttery, garlicky plate of baked, herb-infused snails is great as a forager's starter, and can pack in some real protein when there's not much else about to eat.

In order to make garden snails edible, a 'purge' is recommended first. Snails can pick up unwanted bacteria and contaminants, if not from your garden then from other people's, so it's wise to get rid of this from their intestinal tract first.

To eat, follow this simple recipe and enjoy getting your own back and a tasty protein-rich dish all at once!

Place your collected snails in a large well-ventilated container (a tupperware box with plenty of holes drilled in will do very well) with a few drops of water and a carrot. Be careful not to overcrowd them or they may not survive.

Clean out the container every couple of days until the snail faeces turns from being black/brown to a lighter orange in colour.

In a large pan, bring 1l chicken stock to the boil and then place the snails, shell and all, in the liquid for 10 minutes.

Let them cool, then remove each snail from its shell with a proper 'snail fork' (or a cocktail stick will do just fine), and wash thoroughly.

In another large pan, sterilise the snail shells by boiling them in a strong salt and water solution. This kills any remaining bacteria in the snail shells.

Making the garlic butter: for every 10 snails, use 45 grams of butter as a rough guide. Leave the butter out of the fridge and soften with the back of a fork. Add the herbs and crushed garlic and mash into a paste.

Cooking the snails: put a little knob of your garlicky, herby butter into each shell, followed by the washed snail and cap off with another little knob of butter. Grill/bake the snails with the opening facing up to keep all of the lovely juices in the shell. The French use a snail-baking tray which looks like a smaller muffin tin. An alternative is to use a large stick of white French bread, sliced in half, and then squash the shells into the bread, which will keep your snails upright. Grill them until the butter is melted and bubbling away.

To eat, use your fork or another cocktail stick to remove the snaily goo and *bon appetit!*

[12 SNAILS PER PERSON]

1 CLOVE OF GARLIC PER PERSON
A HANDFUL OF CHOPPED
  PARSLEY
SALT AND PEPPER
BUTTER – ALLOW 45 G PER 10
  SNAILS AS ROUGH GUIDE
1 L CHICKEN STOCK

THE THREE HUNGRY BOYS
BREAKFAST CHALLENGE

IN A LIFETIME, YOU will eat breakfast (assuming you have it every morning for 80 years) 29,200 times. Let's be frank, that's quite a lot of toast and cereal. And as it's the 'most important meal of the day, dear' as my grandma used to say, why not make it a bit more fun?

So here's the Three Hungry Boys breakfast challenge. It's a kind of *River Cottage* meets *Ready Steady Cook* scenario. The breakfast is simple. Eggs on buttered toast, with ketchup. But you have to make it all, from scratch, in an hour. Well, you can leave the egg-making to the chickens. So that's baking a loaf, making butter from double cream, making a quick homemade tomato ketchup and some poached eggs. Start the clock, here we go.

Thomato's Ketchup

9th June '11

BREAKFAST, FROM SCRATCH, IN ONE HOUR!

0-12mins

Start by making your butter. (See Making Butter recipe over the page). Set the solid butter aside.

12-18mins

It is impossible to make a decent loaf of bread in an hour using yeast-based rising. We can, however, make soda bread within this time, so here goes.

Take the buttermilk you set aside earlier from your butter making, and add whole milk to it (if required) to make 300ml of liquid in total. Stir this into 500g of plain white flour. Add 10g of salt and 4 teaspoonfuls of baking powder.

Quickly knead into dough, divide equally in two, shape into rounds, slash a cross on the top (almost half way into the loaf) and throw in the oven for 25 minutes at 200°C.

18-30mins

Take half a litre of *passata* (you can make your own but shop-bought stuff tastes just as good), and add 50ml of cider vinegar, half a teaspoon of celery salt, mustard powder and ground ginger, a quarter teaspoon of mild chilli (flakes or powder) and black pepper, 50g of demerara sugar and a generous squirt of lemon juice.

Place in a pan, bring to the boil, then immediately reduce to a simmer for 25 minutes, until your sauce has thickened but is still pourable.

30-43mins

Head outside to collect your freshly-laid eggs from your rare breed, free-range chickens. OK, get them out of the fridge then!

Mix a little salt with your room temperature butter, which should be soft. Go for the ratio of 1% of salt to the butter weight. So for 200g of butter, add 2g of salt.

Fill the kettle and boil, ready for poaching your eggs.

43-52mins

Take your soda bread out of the oven and place on a cooling rack for 10 minutes.

Check your ketchup is the right consistency and take off the heat.

Pour the ketchup into a glass bottle and allow to cool.

52-60mins

Place the boiling water from the kettle into a deep frying pan and bring to a simmer.

Slice your loaf and place in the toaster.

The list of methods to poach a neat egg is long and distinguished (like my, ahem...) but, in my opinion, forget using vinegar (completely pointless), forget cooking the egg in cling film (it'll come out tasting of plastic), and forget the spinning-water method. My method involves placing the whole egg (in its shell) in the boiling water for 45 seconds, then removing and cracking the egg into the water. This partially boils the egg enough for the white to hold together when cracked into the water. Don't pre-boil for more than a minute though as the white will stick to the inside of the shell. After about two and a half minutes, your poached egg should be ready. Make sure all the egg white is firm and white in colour, not translucent.

Use a slotted spoon to remove the eggs.

Now: set the table, butter your toast, place your perfectly poached eggs on top, with a blob of homemade ketchup and some cracked black pepper, and shout to everyone, 'BREAKFAST'S READY!' What a great start to the day!

MAKING BUTTER FROM DOUBLE CREAM AND ELBOW GREASE

Pour the cream into a large jar making sure not to fill it more than 1/3rd full.

Make sure you tightly close the lid and get ready to put some work in! Shake the jar as hard as you can. The cream will expand first into whipped cream and will probably get stuck round the jar. If this happens remove the lid and spoon the edges to form a ball.

Continue shaking until you can see a single tight ball that should be sloshing about in what looks like milk. This is actually buttermilk.

Drain the buttermilk into a bowl to use later and remove the yellow butter ball.

Squeeze the ball tightly between your hands to expel excess buttermilk then rinse under COLD water to help firm the butter and wash buttermilk from the surface.

Before putting it in the fridge and while the butter is still soft, we like to add some salt to give it flavour; about 1% of the total weight should do it, so in this case 2.5 grams of salt (about ½ a teaspoon).

Place into a ramekin and store in the fridge up to 10 days.

[MAKES AROUND 250G OF BUTTER]

500ML OF FRESH DOUBLE CREAM
½ A TEASPOON OF SALT
1 LARGE JAR WITH TIGHT FITTING LID!

BAKING BREAD

I'VE ALWAYS BEEN A FAN of getting to grips with the basics of a subject first, and then using that platform to experiment a little afterwards. There is no better subject to make this point with than bread baking. So let's start with a basic, yeast-based white loaf. Master it. Get to understand the ingredients, quantities, yeasts, proving times and oven temperatures. And then take it from there. Because there are plenty of options after that!

But why should you bother taking the time to bake a loaf, when you can buy one readymade from just about anywhere? Well, I can only urge you to give it a try – the pleasure to be had from making your own bread from scratch is pretty enormous. That said, if you were to grow all your own fruit and vegetables and bake every bread and cake from scratch, it would be a full-time job – I can tell you that from experience! So while we are huge supporters of doing all these things and incorporating them into your life as much as possible, the straightforward truth is that it's all a balancing act, and only YOU can decide what is right for your lifestyle. But give baking bread a go. I urge you.

BASIC WHITE LOAF

The easiest way to learn and remember a white bread recipe is to talk in percentages relative to the main ingredient, flour. There are only 4 key ingredients so it's really quite simple.

Flour, 1kg (100%)
Water, 580-600ml/g (58-60%)
Salt, 20g (2%)
Dried yeast, 10g (1%)

Flour: a huge array of flours will greet you when you head down the baking aisle or look online, but for this purpose there is really only one option: 'Strong' bread flour. It comes in white, brown or wholemeal but white is the easiest to learn with. The 'strong' part doesn't mean that it can bench press more than Rambo, but refers to the level of proteins in the flour that combine, when mixed with water, to make gluten, a hugely important part of getting a light fluffy loaf. Stick to a 1kg bag of flour, that way it's much easier to remember the ratio 100/60/2/1.

Water: for the purposes of making bread (though not science!), a millilitre and a gram are the same thing, so for every 1kg of flour, we use our handy percentage, and use 600ml of water to give a good, workable dough. Using lukewarm water will speed up the process of yeast activity and is recommended. Just make sure it is not hot water, or the yeast will die and, at best, you will end up with something resembling a rock.

Salt: this is really important, and you must accurately weigh the salt to go in your mix as over- or under-salted bread isn't very nice, and being 'out' by only a very small amount can make a big difference. If you want a low-salt diet, don't put less salt in your mix, just eat less bread. I'm serious; low-salt bread is fairly grim.

Yeast: yeast comes in a few forms, but powdered dried yeast is readily available in most supermarkets, is cheap and super easy to use. When you first start out, don't entertain using any other type.

METHOD

Mix the dry components together well in a large bowl, before adding all the water.

Bring the mix together, until you have one ball of dough and a relatively clean bowl. This should take no more than five minutes.

Now comes the kneading. Place the ball in front of you on a flat, clean surface. Hold the front of the ball with one hand and, using the heel of your other hand, smear the ball into the surface, pushing away from you. Then roll the dough back towards you into a ball, turn it 90 degrees and repeat the process. Do this for 7-10 minutes – the consistency will change as the dough becomes elastic.

Divide the dough into three equal balls for three medium size loaves. (The following steps will need to be carried out on each ball.)

Flatten the ball into a disc shape. Gently lift an edge with two fingers and fold it into the middle. Turn the dough clockwise slightly and repeat the 'lift, stretch and fold' step. Do this 5-8 times until you have gone around the dough ball. Now, turn the ball over. Without this step, you will end up with a heavy loaf that struggles to rise.

Place the dough in a plastic bowl (glass/ceramic bowls can be cold, making the dough take longer to rise), large enough to allow the dough to rise to DOUBLE its original size, and seal inside a black bin liner. The bin liner will help retain the moisture and keep your dough warm. Leave in a room temperature area and it will double in size in 20-90 minutes.

Once risen, tip the dough out onto the work surface and 'knock back' by gently flattening it using your fingertips (this deflates the carbon dioxide bubbles). Shape into a round ball again by repeating the 'lift, stretch and fold' step. You can rise and knock back the dough several times, supposedly improving texture and flavour but we recommend one rise, one knock back and then a final rise (also known as the 'prove') before baking.

Place your dough in a lightly-greased loaf tin. Allow to 'prove' to almost double the original size. Keep a close eye on your dough, as over-proving stretches the gluten fibres to the point where your loaf will collapse, and under-proving will lead to a heavy, dense loaf.

Make sure your oven is as hot as it can be.* Spray the top of your proved loaf with a little water and place a shallow bowl of boiling water at the bottom of the oven (the steam will keep the loaf soft). Three loaves from 1kg of flour will take about 30-40 minutes, but if the crust is browning too quickly, turn the temperature down slightly (to 180 degrees). If you tap the bottom of the loaf, a hollow sound means your loaf is ready. If it makes a heavy, dead sound, bake for 5-10 minutes more.

Allow to cool on a rack and ONLY slice when cooled. Enjoy – it's the best thing since sliced bread!

*When cooking your bread, it is important to get the oven to 250 degrees, or the hottest setting possible. Preheating can be a bit of a waste of energy, so a 3HB tip is to bake your loaf after you have used the oven for something – that way your energy wastage will be kept to a minimum.

MAKING YOUR OWN BILTONG

I FIRST EXPERIENCED THE wonderful South African snack of biltong aged about 13, waiting for a physics lesson. Simon, a sporting South African, joined our class and he quickly introduced us all to the stuff. Biltong is a cheap, easy and exceptionally tasty way of preserving good red meat, and it will take you between one and three weeks to achieve your own perfect stash. It was originally used as a method of preserving red meat when hunters had killed more than they could eat immediately. One story goes that they used to preserve the meat by keeping it under the saddles of their horses, making the meat tender and adding a salty tang (ew!).

My first attempt at making beef biltong was an unmitigated disaster. The key to successful biltong preparation – and where I failed – is to kill any bacteria or fungus in the meat so that it can dry before it is allowed to rot. So, we kill the bacteria by salting the meat first, then killing any remaining bacteria with vinegar and finally dehydrating the meat to make sure bacteria can't reproduce. All of this does a great job at preserving the meat and gives it part of its distinctive flavour. Biltong is pretty low in fat and carbohydrate, and very high in protein, which is needed for loads of things in the body. It has recently become a super food for some celebrities – perhaps they've been watching our programme!

WHAT YOU'LL NEED TO MAKE A STASH OF BILTONG

1KG OF TOPSIDE OF BEEF (ask a butcher if you don't know what this is!) or similar meat (venison would work too)

1 LARGE CARDBOARD BOX

WOODEN SKEWERS

400ML VINEGAR (any type will do – cider/ white wine etc. I use a mix of red wine and balsamic)

SPICES:
50G CORIANDER SEEDS
25G DRIED CORIANDER POWDER
WHOLE PEPPER CORNS, CRUSHED
CHILLI FLAKES

NEWSPAPER/ SAWDUST (something to collect any drips)

A WARM PLACE

MAKING YOUR BILTONG BOX

Draw the net of a box onto a large sheet of cardboard. This is on the KS2 maths curriculum so any nine year olds will be able to advise. Your box needs to be tall enough to let your longest strip of biltong hang but not too wide or your skewers won't reach from side to side.

Cut out the net and stick it together with lashings of gaffer tape.

Take out your frustrations by banging some holes in the side of the box using a knife or pair of scissors, remembering to be really, really careful of your fingers. (These holes are to allow ventilation.)

Check that your wooden skewer will reach from one side of the box to the other. If it doesn't, you'll need to start again with your box, making sure it does. (I've done this twice.) Then pierce a hole towards the top of each end of your box to put your wooden skewers in place – two or three skewers will be enough. You will eventually hang your strips of meat over these.

Add a lid to your box, which you will eventually secure with more gaffer tape. (If you can't get gaffer tape, Sellotape will do.)

Make sure you replace your cheapo biltong box every three batches or so. More for hygiene than anything else.

NOW, MAKING THE BILTONG...

Use the best topside of beef you can find from the local butchers. I use a 'salmon' of topside normally as it's cheaper than rump but has a very good texture for biltong. Supermarkets will sell similar cuts to these but a much better deal is to be had from a specialist butchers on your high street. (There's not too much point in making biltong from the best fillet steak as it's better to eat that cooked!).

Take the meat and cut it into strips about 3cm wide and 1cm thick. Cut with the grain.

Cover the strips in enough salt to completely coat them, including the sides. It's best to use cheap, granulated salt as it gets in all the nooks and crannies and won't make the process too expensive.

Leave the strips for about an hour, longer if you like it really salty.

Pour the vinegar into a roasting dish and gently rinse the strips in the vinegar, again leaving for about an hour (longer if you like it more vinegary).

In a dry frying pan, toast 50g of coriander seeds until they smell buttery and have darkened in colour. Smash them up with a pestle and mortar and add the ground coriander powder.

Remove the beef from the vinegar and dry on some kitchen towel. Cover the strips of beef liberally with coriander seeds and powder.

Liberally rub the crushed peppercorns/toasted coriander seeds/chilli and anything else you like into the biltong and give it a good smash to drive the flavour into the meat.

Hang the meat over the wooden skewers in your well-designed cardboard box, put the lid on and gaffer tape it shut. Find a warm, dry well-ventilated place for your biltong box and leave for about a week, checking every other day or so to make sure the meat hasn't turned green or furry. (In Africa they let their biltong hang on lines outside, covering the meat with a fine, mesh fly-net to keep off any creepy crawlies. Sadly, I think it may be a bit wet in the UK to have strips of meat hanging on your washing line, so inside in your cardboard box is definitely best. And keep the box away from any curious pets, as I'm sure any dog would be very appreciative of the snack.)

After a week, your biltong should be hard where the meat is thinnest and a tiny bit squidgy in the thicker bits, especially if you like your meat a little red in the middle. If it's too red, leave it for another day or so, and cut the strips a bit thinner the next time you make your biltong.

Finally, chew your meat like a dog with a bone. You can also chop it up fine and stick it in a bowl for people to nibble, or blend it and add it to a dish to add extra flavour. I personally like it nice and simple.

JAM

FIRST OF ALL, LET ME set the record straight. Jam making is easy and quick! A lot of people I meet seem to think it takes hours of slaving over a stove, but in actual fact there are quite a few fruits that can be made into jam in 30 minutes – and if you haven't got half an hour to spare to make something delicious, you really are reading the wrong book.

There are only four components you need to understand to make jam. These are fruit, sugar, pectin and acid. It's as simple as that (he says in a confident tone).

1. Fruit

We love strawberry, raspberry, rhubarb, apricot and damson jams, or come to think of it, any fruit that we happen to have plenty of. And you will need plenty – if you want to make more than a couple of jars, you will need at least 1 kg of fruit.

2. Pectin

No pectin, no jam. Sloppy fruit syrup you may have – but jam? No. You see pectin is the ingredient found naturally in many fruits and is the key ingredient (when combined with sugar and acid) to setting and solidifying the whole mixture. If your fruit is low in pectin, either mix it with a fruit that is high in pectin, or use 'jam sugar'(which contains added pectin). Whatever you do, don't use jam sugar if your fruit is high in pectin as the resultant mix will be good for making a cricket ball and that's about it.
Levels of pectin in fruit:

* High: crab + cooking apples, redcurrants, damsons, gooseberries, unripe plums – use regular sugar.

* Medium: apricots, blackberries, unripe cherries, ripe plums, raspberries – use half jam sugar and half regular sugar.

* Low: ripe cherries, peaches, pears, rhubarb, strawberries – use jam sugar.

3. Sugar

In general, if you use granulated white sugar you won't go far wrong, unless your fruit is low in pectin (see above). The other sugars you can use are golden or demerara sugar, but these have a stronger flavour and can mask delicate fruit, like rhubarb.

4. Acid

Acid draws pectin out of the fruit and prevents the sugar from crystallising. In general terms, the acid level is roughly the same as the pectin level in the fruit. For example, crab apples, gooseberries and damsons are high in pectin and acid, and peaches, rhubarb and strawberries are low in pectin, and low in acid. Don't fear though, just as you can obtain pectin from other sources, so too you can boost the acid by adding lemon juice – the juice of 2 lemons for every 1 kg of fruit is about right.

There must be a million recipes out there for jams, so really the choice is yours. Making something a bit different can always be fun, so mixing fruits or adding unusual extras like ginger, chilli, elderflower, or even herbs and spices will enable you set your stamp on a jam. As long as you understand the four key components above, you can make jam, so go for it.

JAM RECIPE

THIS RECIPE USES STRAWBERRIES but the technique is standard, and other fruits can be substituted. Just remember that the correct sugar (or jam sugar) is being used for the fruit, and that there is acid present, either in the fruit or added.

Quarter the strawberries and place in a heavy-bottomed pan. Add the lemon juice to let the acid start drawing out any pectin that is in the fruit.

Add the water and simmer for 10 minutes to soften the fruit and evaporate off some water. You need to lose a bit of the water so that the fruit mix becomes syrupy and the sugar content is at least 60%. Ten minutes is normally about right.

Add the sugar and stir until dissolved, then turn the heat up and boil vigorously for 5-10 minutes. You will know when the mix has reached setting point if you put a few drops on a cold plate and allow to cool (this should take about 30 seconds). Push the drops with your finger and if the surface crinkles, the mix is ready. (Using a cold plate means the mix will cool quickly – if you had to wait 3 minutes for it to cool on a warm plate and you then discovered it was ready, then the rest of the jam would be overcooked.)

When ready, take off the boil before pouring/spooning into sterilised jars – jars (and lids) that are washed, rinsed and then dried in an oven set at 100 degrees will be sterile. Just let them cool a little before filling.

1KG STRAWBERRIES
900G-1KG OF JAM SUGAR (AS STRAWBERRIES ARE LOW IN PECTIN)
A LITTLE WATER, BUT NO MORE THAN 400ML
JUICE OF 2 LEMONS – ABOUT 30-40ML

PICCALILLI

THIS IS AN ABSOLUTE 3HB favourite. The stuff from the shops is generally gooey, with not enough vegetables or spice, so we just had to have a go at making our own. The result is chunky with a kick, and goes down a little too fast. Best made in autumn and served with cold meats, or in a cheese sarnie. Scrummy.

Preparing the vegetables (the day before): Chop up the vegetables into bite-sized or smaller pieces (we like ours really chunky) and place into a large sealable plastic container. Sprinkle over the salt and fill with water to cover. Put in the coriander seeds, whole black peppercorns and bay leaves. Mix together, and then seal. Leave in the fridge for 24 hours.

To make the piccalilli: Make a paste of the cornflour, ginger, cumin, mustard powder and a little vinegar.

Put the rest of the vinegar and all the sugar in a large pan and bring to the boil.

Add the spiced paste to the pan, stir in and continue to boil for a further two minutes, then remove from the heat.

Drain your vegetables and carefully add to the pan.

Stir thoroughly, and then separate into warm, pre-sterilised Kilner jars. If you are using jam jars, it is an idea to use plastic disks with elastic bands to seal, as metal lids can react with the vinegar in the piccalilli.

Seal whilst still hot and label up. Leave for as long as you can stand not to eat it for. We normally eat a whole jar the first day we make it but it's meant to improve with age. Sadly, our piccalilli never manages to get that old.

[MAKES ROUGHLY 4 X 500ML]

YOU WILL NEED TO MAKE UP
  ABOUT 2KG OF VEGETABLES
  FROM THE FOLLOWING:
    CAULIFLOWER
    CELERIAC
    GREEN BEANS
    GREEN PEPPERS
    RED ONIONS
    BABY SWEETCORN
    COURGETTES
BAY LEAVES (ONE FOR EACH JAR
  YOU ARE MAKING)
20G GROUND TURMERIC
1 TSP GROUND GINGER
1 TSP MUSTARD SEEDS
1 TSP GROUND CUMIN
1 TSP MUSTARD POWDER
1 TBS CORIANDER SEEDS
75G SALT
1 TBS WHOLE BLACK
  PEPPERCORNS
50G CORNFLOUR
200G UNREFINED GRANULATED
  SUGAR
1.2 L CIDER/WHITE WINE/MALT
  VINEGAR

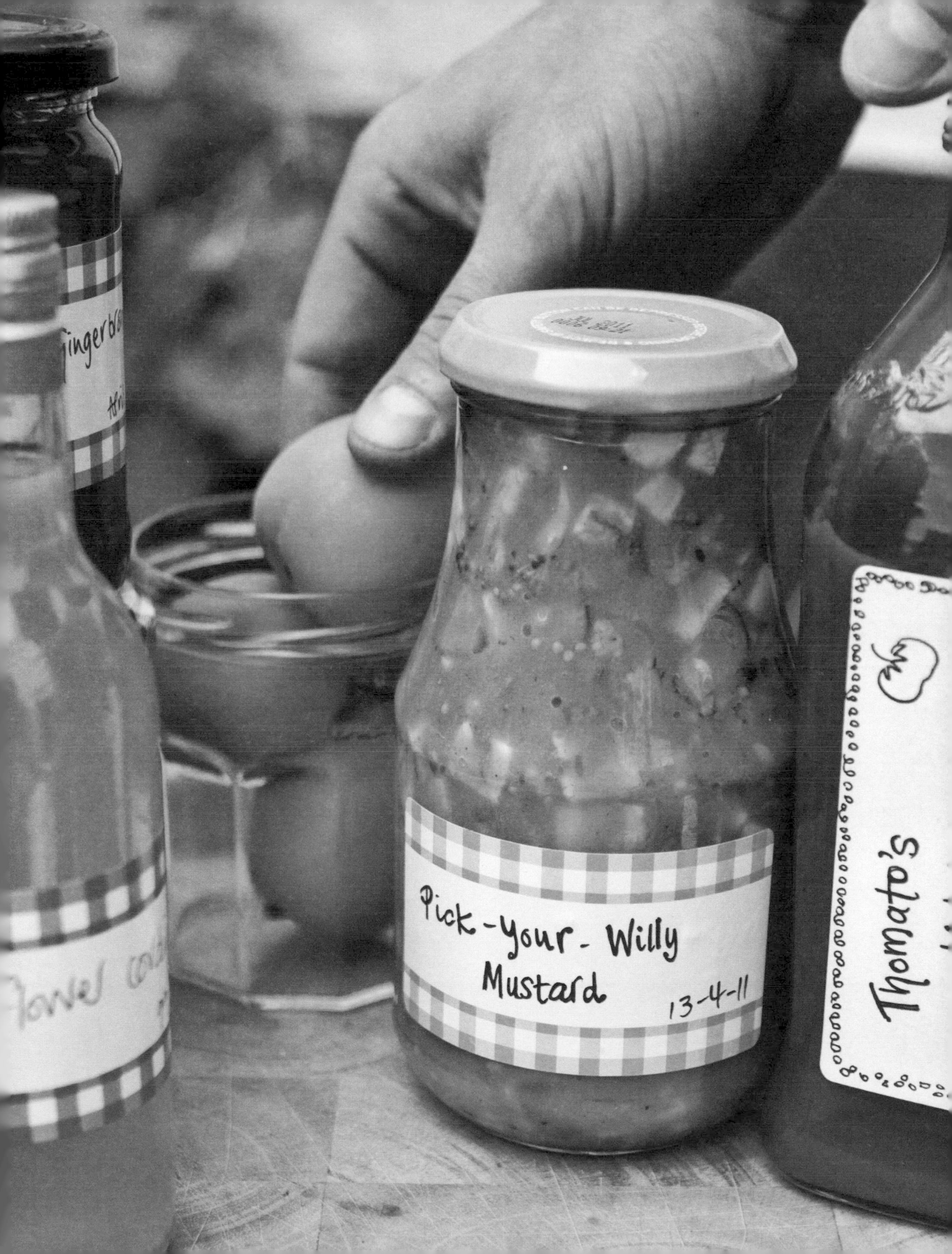
Pick-Your-Willy
Mustard
13-4-11
Thomato's

WHAT TO DO WITH YOUR EXCESS PRODUCE: MARKET STALLS AND PRODUCE SWAPS

IF YOU EVER ATTEMPT TO GROW your own produce, or you have a bumper day of foraging, you might find that you have more apples/chillies/blackberries/plums/mushrooms, than you know what to do with. Mountains of the stuff, to the point where it seems every bowl, cup, rucksack and spare drawer is filled to the brim with Mother Nature's bounty and you're left scratching your head about what to do with it all. Well, the next logical step is to follow some of our preserving tips to make your own jams, pickles, and chutneys. But even then you may find yourself with upwards of a dozen jars of each preserve. And what are you going to do with that? Fill that spare drawer back up again? No! Let's put it to good use.

I'm hoping (and assuming) that if you have followed one of our recipes, you will have ended up with a first-class product that could get you some serious financial investment from *Dragons' Den*, should you have the inclination. But then again, having to explain to an irate Duncan Bannatyne that the rhubarb from your allotment is struggling to make the 3.5 million jars of jam needed for the order he secured at a national supermarket, is not on my top 10 things to do this year... So, we recommend that you keep some jars for yourself, give a few to your very nearest and dearest, and then put all those extra ones to good use and either create a bit of cash, or exchange them for other people's produce.

So here's how to go about it. (By the way, Duncan would never invest in your rhubarb jam anyway. He's much more of an apricot preserve man.)

PRODUCE SWAPS

The internet is great for many things, and none more so than connecting people. Last winter we made some Seville orange marmalade when we found a 1.5kg bag in the reduced section of our local shop for only 49p, which gave us 15 large jars of delicious marmalade. But after having it on toast, roasting chickens and hams in it, and bunging it in a pork stir fry or two for a sweet tang, we had still only made a small dent in our impressive collection. I checked the long range weather forecast and it seemed like we weren't due any floods or snow blizzards to keep us housebound, so we blogged about our excess and offered it up in exchange for other people's homemade produce. We had plenty of interest and ended up with quite a collection of swapped goods, improving our preserves cupboard no end. It is also possible to do this at certain festivals or fairs and I strongly recommend taking an extra jar or two along in the hope you can swap it with other small stallholders (see our Useful Websites at the end of the chapter for more on Produce Swaps).

SET UP A STALL AT YOUR LOCAL FARMERS' MARKET AND GET SELLING

In terms of moneymaking, jams and chutneys must have one of the best ratios of cost to make versus price you can sell them at. Quite often I work out how much each jar costs us and even on the relatively modest amounts we make, it can be as little as 25p per jar. That's pretty good considering you could sell them like hot cakes for around £3 per jar at a local farmers' market. So guess what I'm going to recommend now? Yup, get yourself in contact with a local market and consider bagging yourself a stall for the day. Remember to:

✳ Negotiate hard on the cost of your stall for the day, or offer services such as helping the organiser to set up in exchange for a free stall.

✳ Go for a mixture of produce. There will always be a demand for the classics – think strawberry or raspberry jam and classic chutneys and pickles – then create new recipes that will get you noticed.

✳ Collect and re-use old jars to keep your costs down. Soak used jars in hot, soapy water to soften the labels and scrape them off.

✳ Make them look great. Homemade doesn't have to mean plain jars. Write on some colourful, bordered stickers (in your neatest handwriting) and cut out rounds of bright material to fix over the lid. Dress your jars up so people can't say no to them!

✳ Swap produce with other stallholders. We have swapped pancakes for seafood, chocolate, and lettuces and we have turned lamb burgers into hats and cocktails. Just make sure you have a product that's half decent and you will be fine.

THE ART OF THE BARTER

BARTERING HAS BEEN AROUND for ages, and, in its simplest form, is a great way to get things you want but don't have. Imagine this: you have a plate of delicious strawberries just picked from your garden that you are about to tuck into. There are far too many for you to eat so you wander next door to where Toby the farmer has a herd of cows. He doesn't have time to grow strawberries but what he does do is produce lots of milk and cream. So you offer Toby half your plate of strawberries in exchange for enough cream to cover the rest. He agrees and you both enjoy your lunchtime treat. This, my friends, is bartering; the exchange of goods or services without the need to get money involved.

If you think about the example above, both people wanted something the other had and were happy to exchange. If you bring money into the equation then you start having to think about what things are worth. And this becomes more tricky when people start to make profits and inflate prices to give what is called a 'perceived value' to things.

It's not as if you are new to bartering though. Think back to when you were a kid in the playground, swapping stamps or rubber bands or chestnuts. Maybe you still do it today without thinking, swapping one of your ham sandwiches with a friend's cheese and pickle at lunchtime.

Bartering is exactly what kept us going when we were on our month-long stint in Scotland. In fact, our very first barter was in Oban on the west coast, where we swapped a couple of pollock fillets for a big chunk of beef dripping, which we then used to cook all our food in for the whole month. We walked into a fish and chip shop with our freshly-caught pollock and talked to the owner who seemed a bit sceptical at first but, after we explained what we wanted in exchange, was more than happy to barter.

Of course sometimes you might need to use a confident pitch to persuade someone to barter with you, but that's all part of the process. To make your first attempts a little easier, remember these three key points:

1.
Have a rough idea of what your product or service may be worth before you begin, so that you don't rip someone off or feel like you've been swindled. Aim high and be prepared to negotiate.

2.
Be confident. A lack of confidence in yourself may convey a lack of confidence in your product, so stand up straight, talk clearly and be bold!

3.
Smile and be nice, and be happy with the deal you end up settling on. A good deal is one that leaves both sides happy, regardless of monetary values.

4.
For inspiration, read *One Red Paperclip* by Kyle MacDonald, the true story of how he started with a paperclip and swapped it for one slightly better thing at a time, ending up with a house!

218. URBAN

USEFUL WEBSITES

THE INTERNET CAN PROVIDE lots of useful information on every subject under the sun, but sometimes there are just too many sites on offer for what you need. To help cut down on hours spent trawling Google, here are some of our favourites:

GROWING YOUR OWN

http://www.allotment.org.uk/ This is great for all your home-grown needs, with advice, tips, suppliers and more. Also has useful information on keeping chickens, some great recipes and a month by month guide to what you should be planting and harvesting.

Also: **http://www.vegetableexpert.co.uk/** Great for advice, especially pest control.

And: **http://www.onepotpledge.org/** which campaigns to get people who have never grown anything before to 'give it a grow!'

MUSHROOM FORAGING/ID

http://www.mushrooms.org.uk/ Holds a catalogue of photos of the vast majority of fungi found in the UK. You can search by common name, scientific name, type of habitat, time of year and (most importantly for us!) edibility rating. Very user friendly, a great site.

http://www.rogersmushrooms.com provides VERY detailed lists of thousands of species of fungus. A bit confusing to flick through but great if you want to cross reference or double check the identification of a find.

And: **http://www.wild-food.net** John 'the mushroom' Wright runs foraging courses on mushrooms as well as hedgerow plants/seashore foraging. His wealth of knowledge has taught us a huge amount and his very popular courses can do the same for you.

FREE GOODS

http://www.freecycle.org On this excellent site, people post unwanted goods, in your area, for free. So if you've got a new fridge but your old one still works, post it up and see it go to a good home. You can find everything from kitchen equipment, furniture, clothing, building materials and toys – and, you never know, you might even make a new friend through freecycling.

FREE SERVICES/HELP

http://www.justfortheloveofit.org This is the best way to meet 'like-minded' people in your local vicinity. Sign up and then pick from a long list of things you are either good at, or are willing to do for free. You will then be able to see other people in your area and what their skill sets are. So, if you need help plastering a wall, use the site to find someone with that skill in your area and offer your services in return. It could be dog sitting when they go on holiday, giving them a hand moving house or teaching them to bake the best cookies, it all depends what you can do!

PRESERVING & SMOKING

http://www.coldsmoking.co.uk The best site in the UK for hot and cold smoking tips, covering everything from the different flavours that various types of wood can give, to inspiration on what foods to smoke.

Also: **http://www.pickleandpreserve.co.uk** for tips, recipes and advice when making your own jams and pickles.

6. CAMPSITE

THE BARE BASICS

ALROUGH THE EXACT whereabouts of your trip will affect some of the kit you need, here's a quick guide to the essential kit for living wild.

ONE WEEKEND AWAY: PACKING LIGHT

Multi Tool: we have each have a Leatherman Wave multi tool and they are simply awesome. They have about 10 different functions from knife and saw through to screwdriver and can opener. Everything you need in one little tool. Perfect!

Sleeping bag and roll mat: no one has a fun day when it follows a cold, uncomfortable or damp night. Invest in a decent sleeping bag. You won't regret it.

One man, easy pitch tent: if the weather's OK, this isn't even an essential, but a small, light pop-up tent will keep you dry for a night or two. If a tent is too much to carry, pack a waterproof tarpaulin sheet and follow our guide to building your own shelter to sleep in.

Head torch

Frisbee, ball, or pack of cards: because everyone needs a bit of entertainment.

Sun cream: factor 30. Trust us, you'll regret it if you don't have it!

Waterproof coat and spare socks: warm, fluffy, dry socks at the end of the day are like a little piece of heaven.

Sturdy footwear

Small first aid kit

Water bottle: the essence of all life, humans can go for months without eating, but barely a few days without water. Always carry some.

Spork: a spoon and a fork in one.

Toilet paper: for girls. Boys, just use leaves.

String: how long is a piece of string? No one knows, but a small ball of up to 10m should help you whip a shelter together or fix any breakages.

Fire spark stick: a metal stick and a striker. When rubbed together they create a shower of sparks; hopefully enough to start a fire if you've read our tips!

Insect repellent

ONE WEEK AWAY: ADD THE FOLLOWING TO THE LIST ABOVE, AND YOU WON'T BE ROUGHING IT – ALTHOUGH IT WON'T EXACTLY BE TEA AT THE RITZ

Larger tent: up-size your home.

Table and chairs: for a bit of comfort when eating or socialising.

Cricket set: you're going to be bored with the frisbee after a week. Get into playing the best game on earth!

Cooking equipment: a small portable gas stove, plus basic cutlery and crockery.

Fishing rod/surfboard: you don't have to be any good, but these will help you pass the time on those sunny days or blissful evenings near the water.

Larger torches/gas lamps

Large water butt: saves the hassle of repeatedly visiting the water tap.

Matches/lighter

ONE MONTH AWAY: IF YOU CAN BRING THE FOLLOWING ALONG, ADDING THEM TO THE KIT FROM THE LISTS ABOVE, THEN DO

Duvet and pillows (and even a camp bed if possible): if you're away for a month a great night's sleep will be a priority.

Larger foraging kit: think lobsterpots, and large wicker baskets. You're away for a while so you may as well feed yourself well.

'Proper' plates and metal cutlery

Solar shower: you may be able to get away with a weekend, or possibly a week, without washing. But a month? Forget it!

A Bell Tent: easy to assemble, but with a lot more space inside. You'll appreciate that after a month.

THE PERFECT CAMPFIRE

NO MATTER HOW OLD a man is, he will never tire of starting a fire and turning it into a flaming inferno. It must be the caveman in him. The campfire is also an indispensible part of any camping experience; a good roaring blaze all but guarantees a happy night in the wilderness, and it never fails to bring those sitting around it together.

The most fundamental piece of knowledge you must possess when trying to start a fire is the 'fire triangle'. This consists of 1) oxygen, 2) fuel and 3) heat. If you fail to include one of these, the fire will not start. This is fact. So make sure to remember this.

In this day and age, there are many man-made things available to help you to start a fire – chemical-based firelighters for example – but it is still imperative to know how to build a fire without artificial help. The one piece of equipment you will need is a 'fire spark stick', which you can get from most camping and outdoors shops, costing no more than £5. You can keep it on your key ring and it will mean that you can always make a spark to start a fire – even if it's damp!

Tinder – this is level one of your fuel – it catches alight easily and will help start the fire but will burn out quickly. Tinder can include paper, fine steel wool, and thin, dry tree barks. If you are in a real Bear Grylls-type survival situation, then the three best types of natural tinder available to you are cramp balls, silver birch bark and dry grasses:

✳ Cramp balls are a fungus that grows on dead wood. They are quite common (especially on dead ash trees) and are small, hard, black balls that grow up to the size of an orange. They often appear in groups. Split them open, leave them to dry and they will take a spark very well, allowing you to build up an ember to turn into a flame.

✳ If silver birch trees are around, look for the bark that is dry, flakey and falling off the tree. If you have to prise the bark off it will be too 'green' and therefore damp.

✳ Dry grasses are fairly straightforward! But the fluffy or crispy heads of dry grasses in particular are excellent for starting a flame.

Kindling – this is level two of the fuel, that will burn easily but also for long enough to give heat and flame to ignite your main fuel. Kindling should be dry twigs and sticks, no thicker than your finger.

Main fuel – this is the third level of fuel, which includes larger branches, logs or other slow-burning fuel like charcoal if you are making your fire at home. The main fuel is what gives a good fire depth of heat and will enable it to burn for long periods without assistance.

Each of us Hungry Boys has built a fair few fires in our time. Also, we are a pretty competitive bunch, so we think that our own particular method is the best. So here are three different ways to build a fire. Try each one and see which works best for you – and please let us know who of us deserves to be the winner!

TREVOR'S SURE THING FIRE PLAN

My technique for starting a good campfire is all about not rushing the process and being methodical. I think that you should start off with a good base which is nurtured and allowed to gradually grow at its own pace. Think of it as good parenting; you give the fire a stable environment, all the resources it could possibly need and the time to find itself.

Before you begin you need to make sure the site you choose for the fire is suitable. Ideally you want a surface that is dry and will allow you to make a hollow so that the fire is sheltered from the wind. Wind can be troublesome as too much can prevent you from lighting it in the first place but it can also make your fire burn too quickly which means you will be very busy collecting firewood to keep it going.

You also want to make sure you can return the area to the same state it was in before you got there – so don't try it in the middle of your lawn.

You are going to need kindling first of all, which makes the base of your fire. Then you need to create a dome or pyramid of larger pieces above the base. This pyramid shouldn't touch the base as the idea is that the flames of the base will heat up the pyramid from below

and, gradually, as it gets hot enough, the fire will spread upwards.

You can layer bigger and bigger bits of wood onto your pyramid, but a word of caution. If you put too many layers on, you will prevent air getting to the flames, which is essential in the initial stages. I would wait until you have a good amount of flames and then add the bigger pieces to your pyramid.

Once the pyramid is ready, light the base and look after it for the first minute or so. These first minutes are crucial as fires can be very temperamental at this stage and you need to be on hand to feed it more kindling or light parts that don't catch straight away. Once the pyramid has caught alight, you can then start laying bigger pieces on to it.

The most important part of building a fire is the parading after you have achieved success. You need to let the fire and those around you know who's boss, which is best done by strutting round the fire with your head held high. I really can't stress enough how important this part is – it took mankind thousands of years to learn how to create fire and you have just managed it in a matter of minutes. Well done you. You are very clever. Now make sure that everyone else knows it too. One... two... three... STRUT!

TIM'S 'BETTER THAN TREVOR'S' METHOD OF LIGHTING A FIRE

Trevor will have you neatly placing the logs one by one, and ensuring that you get as smelly and spend as much time by the fire as is humanly possible. I have seen Trevor crying from all the smoke billowing up his nose and in his eyes, and smelt him the next day, when he smells like he's doused himself with half a bottle of the new aftershave 'Smoke', by Trevor. I learned long ago that with good preparation, you

can make a fire burn hot and bright in very little time, using just one match. That's right. One.

You might say: 'But what if you don't have a match or a lighter? Surely you would need two twigs or a flint or a magnifying glass?' Yes, these are all useful in the absence of lighting apparatus but, in all honesty, I have never been in the situation of not having a match. I love Bear Grylls and the other great outdoorsmen, but if I go camping, it is usually a planned thing. Very rarely do I find myself in the Amazon rainforest with nothing but a piece of string and a parachute and so, as I said before, for this fire, you will need just one match (and a box to strike it against).

1. Find dry stuff of various sizes that burns.

2. Dig a shallow hole.

3. In a wigwam formation, build up the dry burnable material, smallest driest stuff at the bottom, biggest dry stuff at the top. Leave a little door to put your match in.

4. Light the small dry stuff at the bottom with your one match.

5. Be smug that in 20 minutes you will have a better fire than Trevor, and you won't smell like Guy on Guy Fawkes' night.

THOM'S BIRD'S NEST AND JENGA METHOD

In my opinion, the most critical thing when building a fire is to have all of your materials to hand from the moment you start. If you start the fire, then have to leave it unattended while you get more kindling or logs, don't expect it to be going when you get back!

So let's assume you've gathered your three types of fuel. Build a jenga-style tower out of your kindling: when viewed from above it should look like the layout for a noughts and crosses game, with the central square being about 6 inches by 6 inches (a nice fit for your burning bird's nest to sit in later) and between 6 and 12 inches tall. This structure will protect the flame from any harsh winds or rain but the gaps between the sticks will allow airflow, a vital corner of your 'fire triangle'. It is also possible to slide smaller sticks between the layers and across the flame, should you need to.

Next, build a 'bird's nest' out of dry grass, thin paper strips or birch bark (or an actual dry old bird's nest if you can find one!) and make it about the size of a large orange. Fluff it up and make sure the driest, most easily combustible material is in the centre. Using your fire spark

stick, strike some sparks on to the centre of a dried 'cramp ball' – if you can't find one of these, the other types of tinder recommended above will do fine. Quite quickly one should take hold and begin to form a small glowing ember. Gently blow on the ember to make it grow larger, then carefully transfer the embers on to your 'bird's nest'. Hold in your hands and continue to blow gently and consistently until the embers grow and the heat gets to the point where a flame is born. Place in the centre of your previously constructed jenga tower and quickly feed it with more tinder to keep the flame going until some kindling begins to take light. Then gradually add the main fuel (being careful not to smother the flame) until, after about ten minutes of tending to your fire, you should have one hell of a good blaze!

Now, all that's left to do is take your shirt off, smear warrior lines on your face, beat your chest and cook the whole woolly mammoth that you caught with your bare hands just that morning. Simple!

BANANA AND CHOCOLATE IN FOIL

NOT ALL COOKING ON A CAMPFIRE is about meat and potatoes. We have a seriously simple recipe for a delicious dessert we'd like to share with you. In fact, it's so simple that we even let Thom have a go at making it.

[FOR ONE SERVING]

1 BANANA
1 BAR OF MILK CHOCOLATE
TIN FOIL

Carefully with a knife make a slit lengthways down the banana, still in its skin. Now push bits of chocolate into the flesh of the banana. Wrap the whole thing up in foil and place into the embers of your fire. Turn the foil package every couple of minutes and cook for about ten minutes.

Remove the foil package from the fire (not with your bare hands, it will be hot!) and open carefully. Allow to cool for ten minutes. The melted mix will be very hot when it first comes out so don't go burning your mouth – we have warned you!

Now just take a spoon and scoop out the chocolate and cooked banana goodness, and enjoy. It's as simple as that.

ALTERNATIVE COOKING TECHNIQUES

WE LOVE A GOOD CAMPFIRE dinner as much as the next outdoor enthusiast but sometimes a bit of variation is needed to spice things up. And that is when we call on one of our alternative cooking techniques. Some of these methods might seem a bit daft but I can assure you, if you put the effort in to test them, the end results will be well worth it.

THE ENGINE OVEN

This one might get you some funny looks while you're preparing it and if you get it wrong will make you pretty unpopular with the car's owner, but if done correctly can be a very effective method of cooking pretty much anything you are willing to try. It uses the considerable heat that a car engine produces to cook your tucker. Obviously you need to enclose your tasty morsels in something otherwise they are going to end up on the A304 and not on your plate where they belong. This is best done using lots and lots of layers of tin foil, and you really, really, really have to make sure your package is 100% sealed. Any juice that is produced from the cooking process will otherwise leak out into your engine, and while your food can probably stand to lose some juice, the car engine is unlikely to benefit from a basting of butter and garlic.

Not all the parts of a car's engine will get equally hot – and you will need the hottest part to cook your food. Usually a spot near the centre of the engine, where the pistons move up and down, is best. If in doubt, run the engine for a bit and feel (carefully) with your hands for the real hot spots. When you have found a good place, wedge your well-wrapped foil package securely in position. It is a good idea to use extra bits of foil around the package to really secure it. Then, set off on your journey and begin cooking.

As for cooking times, this really is down to guesswork. Bigger meals will obviously need longer journeys, so you might need to experiment a little. But imagine the look on people's faces when you arrive at your destination, open your bonnet and pull out a perfectly cooked fish for dinner. That feeling alone is worth the effort of trying this out.

Why not start with a baked potato, and if you achieve success with that, move on to something a little more exciting, like a steak.

THE PIT OVEN

If you want to cook when you're out in the wilderness, your options are somewhat limited, but one great alternative is a pit oven. This is great to use for anything that will benefit from slow cooking, for example bread, or a leg of mutton or lamb.

First of all, dig a shallow hole large enough to fit your pot or cooking receptacle. Then shovel in the embers from your campfire, levelling them out so that you can then place your pot directly on top of the hot coals. Make sure your lid is on very securely. Then fill your hole back up with soil, covering the pot entirely to keep the heat in. Then simply let the embers do their magic. When you think the dish is ready, dig your pot back up and, hey presto, dinner is served.

COOKING ON EMBERS: GRASS-COOKED TROUT WITH MARSH SAMPHIRE

I CAN'T VOUCH FOR THIS recipe as I am yet to try it out but I reckon it will work just fine. The next time we are out camping, we're going to give it a go, and I urge you to do the same. So fingers crossed it'll all go to plan and you'll dine like a king, or it will go horribly wrong and you will be cursing the three of us for being idiots of the highest order.

Prepare your bed of embers and gather lots of lovely, fresh, green grass. Then take your gutted and cleaned trout and stuff the cavity with some wild garlic leaves and butter. (See our guide on how to gut a fish for help with this.) In the summer months you'll be able to find lots of wild garlic – see our foraging section for help on how to identify it.

Place a very thick layer of damp grass on the embers, and then lay the trout on top. Next, cover the fish with another thick layer of grass. Cover the whole lot with a 5cm thick layer of soil and leave for approximately 30 minutes.

Five minutes before you uncover the trout, boil a handful of marsh samphire for a couple of minutes, drain and put to one side.

The trick here is to retrieve the fish without getting soil and ash all over it, so, as carefully as possible, remove the top layer of soil. You should be left with lots of steamed wilted grass covering the trout and protecting it from the heat and soil. Peel away the grass and then carefully remove the trout. Put it on a plate with the samphire, and any remaining butter and garlic can be spooned over the top.

Good luck, and remember, if it goes well and tastes delicious, then I am a culinary hero. If it goes horribly wrong and you end up with a dusty, dry piece of fish, then it was definitely Tim or Thom's fault!

[FOR FOUR]

1 GUTTED AND CLEANED
   WHOLE TROUT
1 LARGE KNOB OF BUTTER
WILD GARLIC
A HANDFUL OF MARSH
   SAMPHIRE

HOW TO BE A REAL GUITAR HERO WITH MINIMAL EFFORT

LET ME START BY SAYING that I am not really a guitar hero. I play in a band where even the drummer seems to be a better guitarist than I am. But I am no slouch either; if I were to use a footballing metaphor, I might be a Denmark or Blackburn Rovers, or Neil Webb from the 1990 England squad. So on these pages, I am going to pass on the meagre knowledge needed to hold your own in a campfire guitar-playing situation – for that moment when, in the flickering light, a guitar is pulled out and all of those around the fire wish that they had listened a bit harder in music class or asked for a guitar for Christmas in 1993, instead of a Sega Mega Drive. If you master these few key points, you can be the musician around the fire and, with a bit of practice, you could even be the next Jimi Hendrix or Rolf Harris. (Probably more Rolf Harris than Jimi Hendrix).

THE GEAR

Guitar

You can spend lots and lots and lots of money on guitars. So much so in fact that my good guitar, the one kept for song writing and gigs and recording and showing off to girls, is worth a considerable amount more than my car. But all of the lovely features of an expensive, super duper, made-from-the-rarest-wood guitar are completely unnecessary for a campfire guitar. In fact, a campfire guitar should be highly disposable and have no value, other than sentimental. You should, in a real emergency, be prepared to take the strings off to use as rabbit snares, use the neck as a club and burn the body for heat.

The best cheap acoustic guitars will sound just fine with a new set of strings and a frequent tuning. You should aim to spend less than £50 and it shouldn't have a name on the headstock that anyone has heard of.

There are basically two types of 6-string guitar in this heady price range: a Spanish/nylon string and a steel string. Generally steel strings will be louder, sound a little better for fireside songs and are easier to restring if you snap them, although nylons are slightly easier on the fingers on a cold summer's evening. I would personally go with a steel string every time.

Guitar strings

Strings come in a bewildering and complex array of thicknesses, materials and gauges. In essence, it is preference that will make you stick to a brand, but they're probably all much of a muchness. You should change strings at least every six months or so or when they start to sound dull. Strings start at under a tenner for a complete set of six: E, A, D, G, B and E. You can get the guy in the shop to change them for you, but it is best to learn yourself, for those moments when you're in full flow and a string snaps. 'Bat out of Hell' just doesn't sound the same without a G-string, so try and cadge a lesson from someone who can teach you – it'll be well worth it.

Tuner

Tuning a guitar by ear is totally possible, but quite difficult. For the purposes of the campfire, investing in a tuner is a good way to go. Again, they can range massively in price but a cheap one will do. The one I use the most cost me 59p and is an app on my iPhone. It is brilliant and is everywhere my pocket goes.

Capo

This is a brilliant little piece of kit and quite often makes an ordinary bit of guitaring sound quite good. It is very simple in essence; by pressing down all the strings on one whole fret it makes the pitch of the strings higher, while still using the same chord shapes. Sometimes, when playing around with chords or a little ditty, it can pay to play the same thing higher up to see how it sounds, which is where the capo can come in handy.

PLAYING CHORDS

Here is a little guide to playing the basic major and minor chords. Remember, your fingers will get tougher in time!

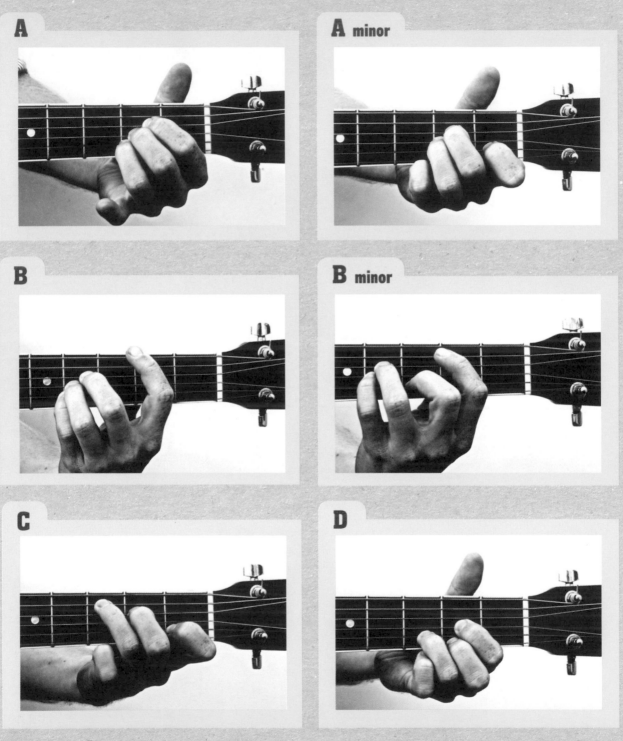

A

A minor

B

B minor

C

D

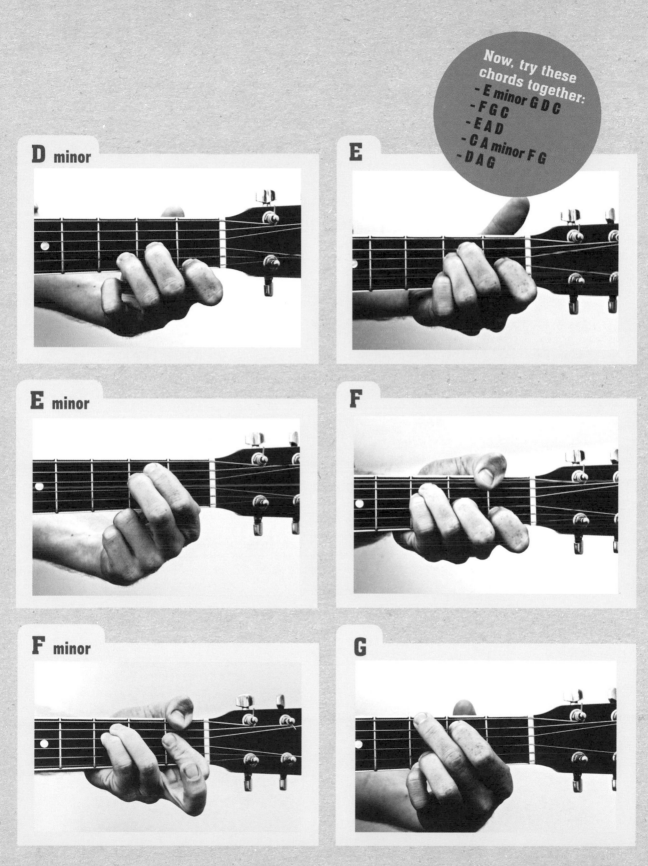

D minor

E

Now, try these chords together:
- E minor G D C
- F G C
- E A D
- C A minor F G
- D A G

E minor

F

F minor

G

TEA

WE LOVE TEA. In fact, at home, we have a whole cupboard dedicated to the stuff. At any one time we usually have a selection that is about 15 strong, although a few of these have definitely earned their place at the back of the shelf for being not that nice/downright disgusting. Oh, and just a note: herbal infusions are not teas!

OUR TOP BLENDS, OUTSIDE THE REALM OF A REGULAR CUPPA:

Earl Grey
Flavoured with bergamot, which gives it a delicate, perfumed, orange-peel taste. Tim's favourite by far. Also try the ratio of 50% normal tea to 50% Earl Grey if you're making a pot. It's great.

Jasmine (with lotus flower)
This is Trevor's favourite. In fact anything with an oriental influence is usually near the top of the list for Trev.

Ceylon & Darjeeling
Both very light and delicate teas, great in the afternoon when watching *Countdown*. Add a crushed sprig of fresh mint for the ultimate in afternoon refreshment.

Rooibos (red bush)
Originating from South Africa, this tea contains zero caffeine so it's great if you fancy a cuppa late at night but still want a decent night's sleep!

TOP TIPS

I'm fairly sure the Three Hungry – or is it thirsty? – Boys possess the World Record (if there is one) for most cups of tea made from a single tea bag. Twelve. Yes, you heard it right, four cups each from a lone PG pyramid. Although we weren't allowed to take any supplies with us on our Scottish trip, I snuck it into my wash bag after liberating it from the hotel we stayed in the night before we started the challenge. To be honest, the last brews weren't much more than hot water with a light brown tinge!

Tea doesn't only make drinks. Try some Lapsang Souchong tea leaves mixed in with your wood shavings when smoking food (see our Smoking Mackerel section on pages 86-87). The unique smoky flavour works very well with delicate fish and also with thinly-sliced hams.

Feeling rough? Sore throat, runny nose and in need of a pick-me-up? Try three thin slices of lemon, a knob of fresh root ginger and 1-2 teaspoons of honey (Manuka honey, if you can afford it!), half a garlic clove (although this is a bit much for some) and a little splash of whisky. Tastes great and I guarantee you'll feel better.

If, like us, you're a tea fan, you could do no worse than checking out The Tea Appreciation Society (**www.lovetea.co.uk**) for organic blends, giant mugs and even fair-trade teashirts (geddit), showing your love for the world's most popular drink.

SHELTERS

THERE ARE SEVERAL POSSIBLE situations you might find yourself in that will require some impromptu shelter from the weather. It might be a fishing trip on a warm, still evening, which persuades you to stay the night. Or your tent might have torn, letting you down when camping, requiring you to think on your feet. Or you just plain feel like you want to connect with nature and you've made an unplanned trip into the wilderness. Whatever your reason, here are some tips to bear in mind when making your shelter.

BEFORE YOU BEGIN

✴ Check the weather. It will be a huge help to know if there is any rain, wind or even snow due! In particular, wind direction, if any, is a very important factor to consider before you start the shelter. You always want the opening of your lean-to to be facing down wind.

✴ Select a suitable site. Look for areas where the ground is dry. Wet areas are a big no-no. Not only for staying dry, but many biting insects breed in wet, stagnant areas and you definitely want to avoid Mr Mosquito if you're after a good night's sleep. Sturdy lean-tos also require some sort of firm structure to build off. This could be a large tree, a dry stone wall or fence. Also look out for animal or insect nests when choosing where to make a camp. The last thing you want to do is spend two hours making a cosy shelter right on top of an ant's nest!

✴ If you are making a fire near your shelter, be aware of flammable items that your shelter is made of or is close to – you want to avoid waking in the night to find your home on fire! (An extra tip is to make your fire and shelter next to large rocks if possible, as the stone will absorb the heat and radiate it back hours after your fire has gone out.)

✴ The best night's sleep will be a bed off the ground in a hammock style sling. No that's not right, the best night's sleep will be at home in your own bed. But the best night's sleep *when camping* will be off the ground on a raised platform or hammock. If you do have to kip on the floor though, a fern mattress is a great way to keep you warmer and drier. Just cut plenty of ferns and/or long grass and lay them in a criss-cross pattern. Not only will this be soft and comfortable, but it will also trap air, a great insulator for keeping you warm.

✴ The size of your shelter should be proportional to the length of time you want to stay. There's no point spending five hours making walls and a roof when you're only going to have one night there. Alternatively, if you are planning on staying a while or you want to re-visit your shelter at a later date, putting time and effort into building it will pay off in the long run.

✴ Knowing the time of sunset is a great help: make sure you have your shelter well built, and fire wood collected before it gets too dark to see. (See our three different methods of making fire for more details.)

MAKING A SHELTER: TWO SIMPLE METHODS.
IMPROVISATION SHOULD BE YOUR MIDDLE NAME...

Shelter Type 1

A rope tied between two trees: you will need a large piece of tarpaulin, some rope and couple of strong trees about 2–3 metres apart. Tie your rope – at a height of 1.5–2 metres off the ground – between the two trees, making sure the line is as taut as possible. Pass your waterproof sheet over the rope between the trees and attach a short (0.5 metre) rope to the brass rings in each of the four corners of the tarpaulin. Now tie the other end of each of those pieces of rope to a large rock or large stick/stake pressed firmly into the ground. This will pull your sheet wide, creating a pitched roof to keep you dry underneath.

Shelter Type 2

A simple lean-to: find some sort of straight, upright, sturdy structure, about one metre in height, which will form the main part of your shelter. This could be an old stone wall, a fence, or large wide tree. Collect at least six strong pieces of wood (with a minimum thickness of two inches) to form the main 'beams' that lean up against the structure, creating a triangle shape to sleep under. Lay other twigs and branches (preferably with their leaves still on to insulate your shelter) in between the beams to give a reasonably solid, sloped pitch that will keep you as warm and dry as possible.

Where you lay your hat

The more adventurous amongst you may well think that a night of impromptu wild camping sounds like a hoot, but let me tell you, you might change your mind when you wake up with a face full of cowpat in a field peppered with rocks. Another risk associated with setting up camp in the dark is that you may find uninvited guests in your bed. Thankfully in the UK there are very few dangerous animals to worry about but our friends around the world are not so lucky. In other faraway countries, there are creatures whose sole purpose in life is to bite, sting and generally make your life a misery. I had a first-hand encounter with one such beast in Thailand and I have to say that, ever since, I have made it a habit to check my bedding for potential hazards before I get in.

The vicious attack took place at night in a hut on the southernmost beach of the island of Koh Tao. After a successful day of scuba diving I had fallen into a blissful sleep, only to be violently woken in the early hours by a stabbing pain between my shoulder blades. I don't know if you've ever been woken up by being stung but it is really, really unpleasant.

I leapt out of bed, taking the mosquito net with me and ending up in a pile on the floor. After I had managed to fight my way out of the net I fumbled around for the light switch to try and work out what had happened. The spot where I had been attacked was starting to really throb, and I immediately started to panic about which kind of deadly spider or snake had done the deed. There was only one thing for it; I had to find the beast, kill it and take its lifeless body to the hospital where they would administer the antidote. I steeled myself and pulled back the covers but instead of a spider or snake in the middle of the bed, there was the biggest centipede I have ever seen. It was the length of a ruler with a dark brown, shiny body. It had more legs than I could count and, in the low light, I thought I could see pincers as long as kitchen knives. We seemed to stare at each other for several heartbeats before the evil creature slunk off, its legs pumping, back into a hole in the floor just visible below the mattress.

I stood rooted to the spot in horror, still trying to take in what I had just seen, when the dull ache in my back brought me to my senses. I stood under a cold shower for about ten minutes hoping this would help, until eventually the pain became bearable and I was left with the dilemma of where to sleep. It was still very early in the morning and I had more diving to do the next day so needed some kip, but the idea of getting back into the same bed was somehow not very appealing. My other options were to go and sleep on the beach, or on the floor but to be honest the chances of meeting more night-time friends was even greater if I did either of those, so in the end I stuffed some t-shirts into the hole, crossed my fingers and got back into bed. I woke the next morning feeling as if my chest was being squeezed by a giant but with no other obvious ill effects.

Ever since that evening, I have had a very thorough check under the covers for creepy crawlies and I suggest that if you find yourself outside for the night, you do the same.

THINGS THAT MIGHT BITE, STING OR GENERALLY MAKE A NUISANCE OF THEMSELVES WHILE YOU ARE CAMPING

JUST WHEN YOU HAVE PITCHED your tent beautifully, lit yourself a roaring campfire, prepared a scrumptious supper, and everything is looking peachy, a buzzing sound followed by a stinging sensation will no doubt come along to ruin your fun. Here's our guide on how to avoid this, and what to do if it's too late.

BEES AND WASPS

Bees die when they sting, and so they tend to try and avoid it at all costs. Their stingers have evolved backward-facing barbs, like those on a barbed fishing hook. When the bee tries to pull the stinger out, it pulls its body apart, killing itself in the process. It's all a bit of a tragedy, especially as the poor bee is only trying to prevent damage to its hive, or protect itself.

Wasps, however, are the spawn of the devil and can seem to attack for no reason at all, other than that they are just a bit annoyed, or have a bee in their bonnet. (Puns stop here.) Wasps have smaller barbs and inject poison from their venom sack with a sawing motion, and with no damage to themselves.

WHAT TO DO: to treat a wasp or bee sting, first, remove the stinger as soon as possible (in the case of a bee sting, a poison sack will also be left behind. Try not to squeeze the sack or you'll be making things worse!) Using a credit card can help to scrape the surface of the skin, whipping the stinger out. Apply ice to the area and leave it for 20 minutes (until melted). This has two effects: numbing the area, which will stop the pain, and vasoconstriction, the narrowing of the blood vessels near the skin which will slow the flow of blood and stop the poison spreading.

Other than the pain, the real danger of a wasp, bee or any other sting is the potential for anaphylactic shock. Anaphylactic shock occurs in very few of the British population, but may come on quickly after a sting. Nearly everyone will react to the initial venom with swelling and pain, but in a person with anaphylactic response, this swelling will spread as the body reacts violently to the invading toxin. Airways may swell up and close, endangering the person's life and potentially causing death. Emergency services must be called immediately if anaphylactic shock is suspected.

It's estimated that without bees, the human race wouldn't survive for more than five years. Bees are essential for pollination of the flowers of many of the plants we need for food. The continuing growth of land development has removed many of the essential natural habitats that bees need to survive and thrive. As such, we see more of them in our own habitats. We can help them out a little bit, by making bee houses and putting them in our gardens. The bee houses give a welcome hiding place for solitary bees on their journey from flower to flower.

MOZZIES – AKA THE MOSQUITO

Mosquitoes can spoil a very nice day. For me, they very nearly spoiled a whole holiday. Whilst in Greece with my family, my brothers and I were stuck in a dingy little basement room with no air conditioning. Our room was conveniently next to a ditch filled with stagnant water, and on the first night the mosquitoes took advantage of our open window. I counted over 150 bites the next day and spent the rest of the holiday either in the pool or covered in stinky chamomile lotion. The point is: the best way to deal with mosquito bites is to not get them in the first place.

WHAT TO DO: Use a repellent spray such as a 30% DEET lotion on yourself, and insecticide such as Permethrin on your gear. Both will stop the mozzies biting but will need reapplying as per instructions. We used Avon's 'Skin So Soft' when we were in Scotland and it seemed to work well. Also:

✳ When sleeping, keep fly nets (and windows!) closed or zipped up.

✳ Keep skin covered with long tops and trousers.

✳ Light a smoky fire – in our experience mosquitoes (like midges) hate smoke.

✳ Find a windy spot. A good, stiff breeze keeps mosquitoes on the ground.

✳ Traditional remedies: ask the locals, they'll often know how best to keep bugs off you and what to do if they bite.

Mosquito bites are also responsible for the transmission of the potential killer disease malaria, which tragically and unnecessarily kills millions each year in developing countries. To reduce the risk of contracting malaria, if travelling abroad to 'at risk' countries, visit your G.P. to get advice on the appropriate course of preventative medication. Go to **www.fco.gov.uk** for more information.

If you do get bitten, to remedy the effects, use:

✳ **Ibuprofen Gel:** to relieve pain and swelling, rub onto the affected area.

✳ **Hydrocortisone cream 1%** gently removes itching and swelling/redness.

✳ **Tea tree oil** – a few drops on the bite area.

✳ **Ice** constricts the blood vessels in your skin and keeps the itchy histamines away (although this might be hard to come by when camping!).

THE MIDGE

It's difficult to do justice to the hell that is a full-on midge onslaught. It's like being at the centre of a flesh-eating tornado. And because they are so small and there are so many of them, the really frustrating thing is that you often don't see them until it is too late. You can't really shoo them off either – and they love getting into your hair.

What to do: Well the best thing is to make sure you are not around midges in the first place, but this isn't always possible. Midges, in some form or other, are found all over the world.

✳ Don't attract them. Midges are primarily attracted to the carbon dioxide humans produce when breathing, so that's quite hard to avoid, but don't leave any car engines running. The less carbon dioxide you produce the better.

✳ Cover any skin you don't want to be eaten. Hats and long sleeves are excellent ideas; bikinis and shorts are not.

✳ Midges seem to thrive in wet areas like marshes and lake beds; you should avoid these if possible.

✳ Midges don't do very well in strong wind, direct sunlight or heavy rain. They are however very good in light drizzle, so days like this become very, very trying as you combine getting wet with getting bitten.

✳ There are numerous repellents on the market, but 'Smidge' is a new product that apparently works very well, and their website also gives a midge forecast and they even have an iPhone app. You can also try eating certain foods to see if that puts them off. Try things like garlic and anything with Vitamin B1 in it – marmite and wheat are good sources.

✳ Some people use midge traps that emit carbon dioxide and have a vacuum that sucks up any midges attracted to it. This is not the Hungry Boy way; we prefer to suffer through it.

✳ Finally, there has been some research that suggests midges favour tall men and big ladies, so you could always try and persuade some people that fitted that description to be your companions, and they could get eaten instead of you.

Winnie

When Thom, Trev and I embarked on our first Hungry Boys adventure we were fairly explicit to Keo Films, the wonderful company that produced the TV series, that we would require some sort of transport for the month, and, given the ridiculous, gargantuan mound of equipment we'd need to survive for that time, it had better be pretty big. A Ford Transporter or an old Mercedes that ran on chip fat would be wonderful. Mates of ours who were in a band had a huge, beautiful van they toured with, which had its own wood burner plus enough space to play a game of twister in. That, we thought, would be wonderful too. But Keo Films had other ideas. As we enjoyed our last 'pre-Hungry Boys' meal of a wonderful slab of fish and chips from a very satisfactory roadside café, we were utterly oblivious to what the crew had lined up for us. In hindsight, we probably should have guessed that the van would be a bit twee, colourful and come fitted with curtains to accentuate our manliness. So, on first meeting Winnie, despite our elation at the prospect of driving an exceptionally cool, brand new, sky blue VW camper, we were worried...

Three guys and half of their belongings take up room. A lot of room. So much room in fact that when packed inside a 1960s-replica T2, bay windowed, water-cooled VW camper van, there is very little space left to do anything else but sit. There is certainly not room enough for two fairly tall guys and one slightly shorter (but equally handsome) man to lie down. But lie down we did.

Our routine involved removing everything from inside Winnie each night and piling it up in a big heap on the ground outside. This – only just – allowed enough room for Thom and Trev to share a 'double' sofa bed in the main compartment and for me to sleep in the pop-up roof. May I add that the roof, although looking roomy and cosy, was in fact designed with children in mind. I'm not that tall, but I am certainly taller than was comfortable for the use of the roof. I was also frequently able to count over a hundred midges, moths, flies and daddy longlegs whizzing around the internal light, as I struggled to sleep, folded up like an anchovy in a tin in my roof compartment.

Moaning aside, all three of us fell completely and utterly in love with Winnie and were very sad to give her back to her owners at the end of the trip. Just as with any good relationship that one day must come to an end, her little quirks and idiosyncrasies were what we ended up missing the most. I would also like to take the opportunity to apologise to the owners of Winnie for returning her not quite in the state in which she was lent to us. There were certainly less curtains, and we may have left her a picnic set or two lighter... Oh, and I'm sure the smell came out just fine, eventually. (That was Thom.)

Winifred is a Danbury replica 2008 1.4l T2 VW camper built in Brazil and is still roaming the British countryside without us. Long Live Winnie.

YEAR PLANNER

JANUARY

Look out for Velvet Shanks when foraging

January 31st: partridge, duck, goose shooting season ends

Look out for Seville oranges for home-made marmalade

FEBRUARY

Look out for Alexanders when foraging, they are young and tender

Plan your vegetable patch

MAY

Elderflowers blooming; get your cordial made!

Crayfish will be out in numbers from now until October

JUNE

16th June: coarse fishing season begins

Start harvesting what you planted in March

SEPTEMBER

Best mushroom foraging months from now until first frosts

September 1st: partridge, duck and goose shooting season begins

Pick your sloes for sloe gin

OCTOBER

Great month for wild swimming in rivers if there has been plenty of rain

October 1st: pheasant shooting begins

MARCH

15th March: coarse
fishing season ends

Many trout fisheries open

Begin first sowing of seeds, and
grow in greenhouse/on windowsill

APRIL

Start planting out your young
seedlings (after last frost)

23rd April: St George's Day;
look for St George's mushrooms

30th April: red stag season closes

JULY

Begin second sowing of plants in
your patch for harvest in Sept/Oct

Make jam with any leftover
fruit harvested and get down
to your local market!

Get out and catch a mackerel

AUGUST

Great Giant Puffball month

August 1st: red stag season starts

Hopefully warm and dry – great
for wild camping and also for
spear fishing as sea temperature
is at its highest

NOVEMBER

Wood Blewits arrive, later
than most mushrooms

November 1st: hind/doe
stalking season begins

DECEMBER

Pike fishing at Christmas,
as long as the water isn't frozen

Look out for Velvet Shanks

Make your own chilli-infused
olive oil from your harvested
chilli plants: an excellent,
cheap Christmas present!

INDEX

ACKNOWLEDGEMENTS

Huge bundle loads of thanks and love to those who have helped me achieve the most wonderful life that puts me in a position to write this. To the family: Mumbles and Pops for your undeterred support in youth and continued belief in adulthood; to Benny and Rupes for being the best two brothers a man could possibly have, I love you both forever; to Livvy for being amazing, putting up with me daily, and baking amazing cakes; to Aud, Hal, the Sterlings and the late Norm for showing me the musical way and much more; to all my Plymouth, Reading and elsewhere friends, to each of you for being awesome; to the staff and students at SDCC who are always supportive; to P and L at Clash & Clash for your understanding; to all at Keo Films, River Cottage and Short Books for your guidance; to HFW the inspirer, and, finally, Trev and Thom without whom I'd probably be a little more hungry.

TIM.

I'd like to thank all my family especially my Dad and big bro Andy. Special thanks goes to my girlfriend, the beautiful Claudine, and to all my close friends; in particular Alboy – we'll win the Marlin World Cup one day! The last year or two have been tough (healthwise) so let this book mark a turning point towards a long and smiling future. And lastly, a massive thanks to the other two T's – One Hungry Boy would just be rubbish.

THOM.

A huge thank you to my family and friends for their support, and at least pretending to be interested in what I was writing. To Hannah, my beautiful and hugely knowledgeable girlfriend, thank you for your patience and advice, I promise it will be worth it. Many grammatical faux pas were averted thanks to you, and any that remain are only due to my perseverance in having them included. For all those that have been involved in the Hungry Boys process: Hugh, Andrew, Zam, Craig, Maddie, Trevor, Tom, Graham, Kate, Callum, Tom, Fred, Cleo, Mark, Vanessa, Aurea, Rebecca, Georgia, thank you – none of this would have been possible without you. Keo Films, Short Books and River Cottage helped send us on our way, so thank you for that and here's hoping there is plenty more to come. And, last but not least, a huge thanks to the two other Hungry Boys for being such good friends. I wouldn't want to explore and adventure with anyone else.

TREVOR.

First published in 2011 by
Short Books
3A Exmouth House
Pine Street
EC1R 0JH

10 9 8 7 6 5 4 3 2 1

A CIP catalogue record for this book is
available from the British Library.

ISBN 978-1-907595-17-2

Printed in Great Britain by Butler, Tanner
& Dennis

Design and art direction: Georgia Vaux

Photo credits:

p. 12, David Attenborough © Ben
Osborne, Nature picture library

pp 12, 29, 56–57 , 58, 68, 72, 115,
117, 128–129, 133, 171, 186–187,
196, 211, 215, 228, 231, 236, 246 ©
Shutterstock Images LLC

p. 149 by kind permission of Ardalanish,
Isle of Mull Weavers

pp 65–66 © John Martin

pp 4–5, 15, 18-19, 48-49, 73, 75, 76–
77, 89, 95, 146–7, 169, 234, 243, 247
& back cover image © Pascal Bergamin

p.7 © Nick Jones

pp. 20, 93, 111, 118–119, 154–163,
164–168, 220–1, 241 © Thom Hunt

All other images © Tim Cresswell

Every effort has been made to obtain
permission for material in this book. If
any errors have unwittingly occurred, we
will be happy to correct them in future
editions.